THE BEARS AND I

The moving story of Robert Leslie, who went prospecting for gold in the Canadian north woods—and found fatherhood!

Adopted by a trio of orphaned bear cubs, Leslie describes their "growing up" together over a period of three years . . . a continuing adventure with perilous canoe trips and a forest fire.

Here is an unforgettable experience in the relationship between man and his fellow creatures. Like *Born Free* it is an important message of hope for preserving the wilderness and all its inhabitants.

THE BEARS
AND I

Raising Three Cubs
in the North Woods

Robert Franklin Leslie

BALLANTINE BOOKS • NEW YORK

To my wife,
Lea Rochat Leslie

CONTENTS

The Bears and I

1

Adopted by the Bears

On the globe, the Fifty-fifth Parallel forms the exact geographic belt line of British Columbia. As the imaginary divider traverses the center of the province, it crosses Babine Lake, a meandering body of delphinium-blue water up to five miles wide and 125 miles long. For more than three hundred miles, the lake's canyonlike coastline—a shadowy green wall of coniferous forest in every direction—rises in rolling, majestic sweeps toward the massive Babine Mountains. Rounded or flattened along their crests, the summits appear less lofty than they really are because their bulk is softened by the all but impenetrable wilderness of second-growth fir, spruce, balsam, and hemlock.

Its southernmost arm running almost due east and west, the lake becomes wider as it spreads through seventy miles of sprawling canyons and upland moors. Beyond the Big Bend, the great northern forefinger points straight north for the final thirty-five miles. In sharp contrast with its austere, if not somber, north-woods setting, a narrow band of bright, crystalline beach that sparkles even on cloudy days separates the dark-green forest from the dark-blue water. From the shoreline, Babine Lake gives the impression of a wide, still, endlessly winding river.

A day and a half by canoe—provided the headwinds were on holiday—north of the trading post of Topley Landing, my Beaver Indian friend, Red Fern, owned a large, comfortable log cabin that perched like an eagle's eyrie above the south bank of Nugget Creek on the western shore of the lake. During lengthy

1

northern summer sundowns, I used to stretch out on a hammock between two lodgepole posts of the sitting porch and watch moose and bear swim back and forth across the lake. While Red Fern was away for the summer, logging for the sawmill people at Pendleton Bay, he allowed me to use the cabin in return for a quarter of whatever gold dust I could pan and sluice from Nugget Creek. I was trying to earn a "stake" for college. We called the operation "sharecropping a claim." Other Tahltan, Babine, Sekani, and Kasha Indians worked legal claims near the northern extremities of the lake, and their dugout pirogues, Hudson Bay bateaux, and Peterborough canoes occasionally plied the windy water between their summer "diggin's" and the trading post where they weighed in their meager endings against "belly-wash" (black rum), sour dough starter, food staples, tools, jeans, and other necessities they were unable to wrest from the forest. During winter months most of the young men tended traplines or felled timber for the lumber outfit near the Landing. Older folks sewed moccasins from tanned moosehide or shaped and laced the world's finest rawhide-on-birch snowshoes (bear-paw design), which they used as summer currency at the Hudson's Bay Company in Prince George.

One afternoon in late June I was spinner fishing from a rocky point that jutted out where Nugget Creek entered Babine Lake. The air was alive with gossipy, late migrants—songsters that arrived each year after the waterfowl. Two loud-mouthed white hunters in a skiff with a cranky outboard clattered by on their way out of the "bosquey"—Chinookan-Keresan jargon for wilderness. The breeze caused a rippling surface movement on a huge, furry mound amidships—silent testimony to successful bear hunting. Whether fishing, hiking, or panning the stream bed, I was always conscious of nearby black and grizzly bear, elk, deer, and moose. An Indian guide from Burns Lake had brought in at least two parties of trophy hunters and fishermen that summer.

The skiff had barely rounded the point of land that extended into the lake like a short peninsula, when three black bear cubs, no larger than a child's teddy bear, and a scrawny old she-bear panted out of the timber north of the mouth of Nugget Creek. The four ran down the beach, splashed across the shallows where I was fishing, and begged me for my catch. The hunters were still in sight.

"Get back in the woods, you stupid fools!" I shouted. "Can't you smell what's in that boat?"

Frightened by my arm-waving and the tone of my voice, the bears took temporary cover in the willow scrub a few yards up the creek. From the amount of thrashing around and squawking coming from the brush, it was plain that the old female was coping with a compound disciplinary problem. I realized the wind favored the riflemen should the animals expose themselves.

Wet and exhausted, the triplet cubs finally accepted safety ninety feet up the lichened trunk of a giant fir that had grown for centuries at the brink of the cliff on my side of Nugget Creek. From their perch on a branch that overhung the creek, they watched the old bear crouching in the understory of willow and alder. Each time I threw her a fish the cubs would wail, hungrily, with a raucous, throaty sound not unlike "Maw! Maw!" She refused to let them descend.

Making the most of an especially eager run of rainbow trout which I planned to cure with aspen leaf smoke and maple charcoal in Red Fern's smoke shed behind the cabin, I continued to fish until sundown. Aside from an occasional glance up the trunk of the old fir at the edge of the bluff, I paid almost no attention to the three puffy little black bumps whining on the branch.

That evening as I sat on the top step of the porch, smoking my pipe and squandering an hour on the twilight view, I wondered why the cubs didn't come down and run away to where little bears and their elders were supposed to run. However, it was certainly no affair of mine, and I wasn't about to interfere.

The gentle old female was no stranger. For the past two summers I had put out scraps for her. I knew she was much too old to be the dam of those cubs. Their

mother had been shot. The older female had adopted
the orphans, as is almost always the case up here in
the northland when little animals are abandoned. But
she was an old bear, rheumatic, slow, and far beyond
the age when time deprived her of the patience and
endurance needed for a two-year responsibility for
three youngsters.

Triplet cubs are smaller than twins and remain
dependent upon a mother through one hibernation
period beyond their yearling winter.

How many times, during the more than thirty intervening years, have I recalled what that venerable
old she-bear did next! Almost on her belly, the scarred
veteran timidly and slowly approached the porch where
I sat. With a look of anxiety I had never before observed in a wild animal's eyes, she sat down on the
grass directly in front of me at a distance of six feet.
Moving her head slowly back and forth while gargling
out purposefully soft tones that seemed to form deep
within the cavern of her throat, the bear impressed
me as if she was trying to convey some message across
that insuperable barrier between man and beast. It was
obviously a subtle plea that had nothing to do with
panhandling food scraps; yet because of preconceived
negative images of beggar bears, I hardly believed,
at first, that I could possibly interpret her supplication.
Never for a second did I take my eyes from her. It
was not that I distrusted her; she had simply aroused
my mild, if imperceptive and unintuitive, curiosity.
During her strange behavior, she often shifted her gaze
between me and the well-treed cubs, soon leaving me
little doubt that her message concerned the little ones.
Finally, after a lengthy, searching stare, she dropped
her lower lip below the gumline, mumbled a few
pathetic whines, got up, then staggered stiffly toward
the game trail that led into the forest behind the cabin.
From all outward appearances, she was abandoning
the desolate cubs.

The moon rose over the Ominecas to the east and
sent its long, sparkling shaft of yellow gold across the
lake. A distant timber wolf howled and received an
answer. A moose trumpeted for his mate. It was almost

10:30 P.M.; the sun had dropped briefly behind the Babine Mountains where it would creep around to the Omineca Range and rise again at 2:30 A.M. Under normal atmospheric conditions, sunset up here in the summertime was divided into two periods: the amber hour and the red hour. In June the nights are only about four hours long. That evening I retired before the end of the amber hour, but somehow I was unable to dismiss those three cubs from the quick of my conscience. Supposing the little fellows were hungry! I hoped they would make it easy for me by being long gone with the old bear come morning.

The sun was still below the toothy rim of the Ominecas east of the lake country when I hurried guiltily from the cabin and headed straight for the big fir at the rim of the cliff above Nugget Creek. Three pairs of shiny little black beads peered down from three balls of fur on the first branch. The diminutive creatures had moved to within thirty feet of the ground to spend a more comfortable night on the flat shoulder of the tree's huge right arm.

Returning to the kitchen, I cooked a big pot of cornmeal mush, stirred in a pint of honey, added a can of evaporated milk—all precious commodities that had been hand paddled by canoe along a three-day windy piece from Topley Landing to the Nugget Creek cabin. Having dished up the concoction into three heavy soup bowls designed for hefty, if nonfastidious, northern appetites, I placed the banquet near the bole of the fir and stepped back toward the porch to await the inevitable.

The fragrance of warm cereal, honey, and milk immediately reached the sensitive little black snoots of the cubs. They began an endless argument that included whining, cuffing, hissing, snarling, and snapping. None of the three wanted to be first to violate the old bear's edict to remain treed; none dared slide down that trunk and eat in front of the bearded stranger; so the cereal was cold by the time the noisy trio finally succumbed to the elemental urge.

Without taking their eyes from me for a fraction of a second, the foundlings slurped up their breakfast in record time, licked the bowls clean, then rebounded to the reasonable safety of their limb.

After refilling the bowls—this time with dried prunes, a criminal extravagance—I resumed my placer work. Shoveling sandy muck into the long sluice box, then opening the floodgate to direct the current through the trough, I removed the heaviest gravel by hand. When all the mud had washed away, I sluffed the remaining sand over baffle-fingers for inspection of the pavement of galvanized metal riffles to see if any flakes of gold had been trapped during the tedious, laborious operation. On top of the long, perplexing hours he spends in loneliness, frustration, and back-breaking work, the placer miner is constantly wet and eternally exposed to sun, wind, rain, and ravenous bugs. Days sometimes drag into weeks without a trace of "color" in pan or sluice to pay for the onerous labor.

By seven o'clock that evening I had earned less than a dollar. My thoughts divided between the poverty of Red Fern's claim and a touch of homesickness for my parents and home in southern California, I had all but eliminated the bear cubs from my thoughts. Climbing the path between the stream and the cabin, I became vaguely aware of being pursued. Whirling around faster than is wise when followed in the north woods—fast movements can be misinterpreted and cause a moose or a grizzly to charge—I discovered the three cubs timidly tiptoeing along the trail in single file behind me, their clamshell ears flattened back like those of collie pups. As I passed the fir I picked up the empty bowls and proceeded to the cabin. The bears tagged along at a discreet distance, mumbling some kind of running, underbreath argument that sounded halfway between a squeak and a grunt. I can still see them as they sat down and formed a neat row on the edge of the porch, hung their heads, and looked silently up at me with that pathetic and unmistakable appeal for help universal in every orphan who realizes his plight.

For a starter, I went to the smoke shed and withdrew three large rainbows. Placing a fish across each bowl, I arranged the receptacles near the steps and far enough apart to preclude certain issues of ownership which I felt must now and then arise among teddy bears. With the delicate manners of a gourmet, each youngster approached his bowl, sat on his haunches, embraced the large trout, and systematically devoured the succulent fare *à la babinaise.*

Although they appeared less frightened than on the previous evening, they eyed with deep suspicion every move I made and jumped with a hair-trigger start each time I changed my activity; still, they showed no inclination to leave.

Without formal invitation or enticement, I left the cabin door wide open while I was inside preparing my own bannock and baked squaw fish. Soft mutterings, often punctuated by sharp, drawn-out whines, indicated a weighty discussion in progress on the porch. When I heard no more of the guttural debate, I turned from the kitchen to investigate. The cubs sat tightly clustered on their haunches, clinging to each other with their forepaws, and staring at me from the frayed remnant of carpeting in the center of the living room floor.

Red Fern's cabin of heavy, peeled spruce logs had two rooms: the kitchen and a living room. He had built bunk beds along the walls at one end of the spacious "parlor" near the cobblestone fireplace whose width spanned most of that end of the cabin. Years later the lean-to kitchen, with a cellar below it, had been added to the south side of the original building as an after-thought when Red Fern married a widowed Sekani squaw who refused to live in a house without a kitchen, a frost-proof cellar, and a cast-iron cookstove. In contrast to the cabins of most northern Nadene Indians, the wall along the front porch consisted mostly of window glass. By framing the door between the windows and the front ridgepole supports, Red Fern had gained added structural strength often overlooked by more hasty cabin builders. He liked the view of the lake during all seasons; therefore he had built the dwelling so as to reap the greatest poetic harvest of the natural beauty of its setting regardless of season. I found it too much of a chore to keep condensation and frost wiped and scraped from all those windows.

A cloud bank, moving from the Yukon down the western slope of the Rockies, had shoved in a cold, arctic air mass; so I kindled two dry logs in the fireplace, lit a coal oil lamp, pulled up a deep, moosehide chair, and settled back to spend an evening with the rousing works of Robert Service. The cubs looked deathly afraid of the crackling fire, but curiosity—an ursine characteristic—soon overcame their fear. Emboldened, no doubt, by full bellies and the warm, friendly surroundings, the feisty little creatures crept closer and closer to the cheerful flames, only to be driven back squealing into dark corners under the beds when pockets of trapped gas along the sides of the logs would explode with loud reports and blinding showers of sputtering sparks.

If they were frightened by the fire, the cubs were mortally terrified by me. They weren't even remotely curious about me as another animal, nor would they allow me to make so much as a step in their direction without bolting en masse beneath a bed. The disappearance of their mother, then their stepmother, must have been still too fresh in their confused little brains. Somehow they connected my species with those unhappy disappearances.

The job of feeding and protecting triplet cubs is more than half again as hard as caring for two, because triplets are smaller and more delicate. Often one of three is sickly, another temperamental, while a third may relish overprotection to the point of ending up too shy to face a bear-eat-bear world on his own. Generally certain natural differences, not apparent in twins, show up in triplets' size, color, and habits.

The trio that stayed with me seemed to be exact carbon copies until I knew them a little better. One was a fraction larger and, instead of being true blackish brown, was actually a burnished rust with a small white spot on his chest. I called him Rusty, partly because of his dark cinnamon color, but also because of the high-pitched squeak which punctuated his leadership when he ordered the other two around.

Immediately upon leaving the cabin after their first night indoors, Rusty snapped at the hocks of his brother and sister until they shinnied up the fir. He wanted to be sure it was safe to explore the clearing behind the cabin. His short grunts soon brought them sliding down when he discovered he lacked the nerve to face the mysterious back yard alone. As they slowly sniffed about, stifflegged, through the weeds of their new terrain, Rusty's squeak, like an off-key willow whistle, was their cue to fall back when they ventured ahead of him. On occasions of dissidence, he stood on his hind legs and fortified his authority with well-aimed right and left uppercuts to the jaw of the dissenter.

The smallest cub was almost solid black, less noisy, and inclined to follow either Rusty or his sister. He bumped awkwardly into everything he passed. He rarely did anything—even eating—without first sitting down to scratch his head behind the ears. It was this act that suggested the name Scratch.

The middle specimen was a bit daintier, measurably less clumsy than her brothers, but none the less a tomboy. On the tip of each hair of her coat was a speck of gray which made it appear as if she had just rolled in the dust. Anyone who has been in the north lake country of British Columbia knows there is no dust in that land of dense forests, sapphire lakes, and crystal shore-lines. Nevertheless, I couldn't resist calling the little female Dusty.

I sensed that Rusty, Dusty, and Scratch might alter my rather casual and totally independent routines as a placer prospector, but I never expected the extent to which those alterations ultimately reached. As we adapted to one another, however, I finally recognized that the bears made more concessions that I did.

At about six o'clock every afternoon of that first week, the old bear came to the edge of the forest, called the cubs, held a hasty conference, sent them back to the cabin, then trundled away up the game trail that followed Nugget Creek into the vast Thomlinson wilderness. After the seventh day, we never saw her again.

I didn't honestly attribute much significance to the old bear's visits until a Chilcotin Indian log skinner by the name of Charley Thwaite docked his launch at Red Fern's landing and came up to the cabin to spend the night. Prospecting for gold and platinum placer along the Babine and Driftwood Mountain streams and lakes, I had enjoyed a lengthy association with numerous backwoods Indian families of the several Nadene tribes. These uncomplicated and often primitive forest people of utter integrity not only taught me their survival woodcraft and loaned me their cabins and tools, but often brought in my food supplies over a hundred-mile chain of stormy lakes and treacherous white-water rivers, then showed me where to dig and pan for the precious metals. Even during the thirty-five months when I lived almost as an animal with the bears—a deplorable estate in Beaver and Sekani eyes —the Indians overlooked my foreign conduct, dismissed it as caused by a complex they could never understand. Charley Thwaite was the first person to whom I related the events of the week.

"Even a mother bear who for some reason abandons her cubs," Charlie said, "will often appear and nose around the new mother that adopts 'em, to check on the cubs' welfare. Indians say the real mother will take 'em back if she's not satisfied. You seem to have passed the test, Bob. Now what're you gonna do?"

"Do I have any choice?" I demanded. "It's just as if Mother Nature herself decreed that I should raise these cubs. I can't run them on to the cougars and wolves and lynx."

"I see big trouble ahead," he warned. "Big trouble for you *and* the bears. Man can't live like a bear. A bear can't live like a man."

The cubs refused to leave the tree until Charley departed next morning.

It was not until the ninth evening in front of the wide-mouthed fireplace that I learned what little bears require beyond food, shelter, and protection. Supper was over, dishes were put away, and I was rereading *The Ballads of a Cheechako* for the fifth time in front of the crackling logs. A steady patter of rain drummed upon the wide-shake roof. From his rug near the hearth, Rusty continued to scruntinize me as he had done from the creek bank most of that day. Dusty and Scratch were enjoying a cuddle and snooze, one on either side of the bigger cub. At length Rusty got up and flatfooted deliberately almost to my chair, at which rashness each of the other two opened one eye and looked. Having sniffed my steaming socks, he stood up on his hind feet, strolled cautiously over to the chair, and placed both front paws on my knee. I decided to ignore him at least for a while, but like elephants and boa constrictors, bears are among the hardest animals to ignore, especially when hungry for affection.

Digging his claws into my leg to summon attention, he stood there quietly staring up at me. Fully erect and reaching up with his paws, the cub measured twenty-two inches from the bottoms of his heels to the tip of his muzzle. Slowly I placed my open palm in front of his nose. I was surprised at the roughness of his long, slender tongue when he licked my fingers. I ran my hand across his neck and shoulders. It was the first time I had touched one of the cubs. I was momentarily shocked at the coarse texture of his coat. As I scratched his puppylike head and held my hand between his big, round ears, the little fellow leaned back to ask for a helping hand to pull himself up into my lap where he turned around several times, then finally lay down in a position from which he could study my expression. Assured by an exchange of wheezy grunts with his brother and sister that his rash act would precipitate no dire consequences, he emitted a deep sigh that caused him to shake all over.

In amazement at Rusty's gall, Dusty and Scratch turned their heads from side to side. Dusty's reply to Rusty's grunts, after studying his impulsive deed, was to amble over to the chair, climb my leg like a monkey, and stake her claim on one third of my lap.

Halfway over to join his siblings, Scratch paused long enough to sit down and rake his scruff as if the act followed consequentially any decision whatsoever. Robert Service fell to the floor; reading was precluded for the night. Each cub outdid the next in establishing a pattern of desirable manners; and as we studied each other's expressions, I sought with equal humility in each pair of questioning eyes an equal quotient of approval. Of one thing I became certain: during those precious hours, rapport and understanding between man and bear were born. No matter what time might bring, all of our lives were henceforth immeasurably affected by the unspoken pact of friendship that night.

Inasmuch as I had assumed the responsibility for raising those bears, I resolved to exert the utmost care against any act that might foist domestication upon them. Such human institutions as rewards and punishment, trained routines, dog-and-master status, and blind obedience seemed in conflict with genuine mutual respect. As a child I had learned from my own Indian father that threatening an animal or inflicting any form of physical pain teaches him nothing, but rather strengthens the characteristic one is trying to correct.

My father, a Cherokee, lived much of his youth in close association with the Jicarilla Apaches near White Oaks, New Mexico, in the 1870's and 1880's. Although his elders moved to west Texas, where he married and began a family of his own, his early Indian training in woodcraft and animal lore remained the dominating influence during the rest of his very civilized life. I was eleven years old when my parents bought a country home in California in the foothills of the Coast Range north of Santa Barbara. Summer and winter alike, my father took his three sons on back-country treks where he taught us the ways of his ancestors. My Scottish mother demanded equal time when we were at home.

Uppermost in my commitment for the next many months with the cubs was the direction of their every activity toward developing self-sufficiency in their own natural habitat, where they could flourish after my return to California. They had to learn nature's laws beyond the jurisdiction of simple instinct, for she rapidly exterminates any species that ignores or violates her complicated code.

Without forcing extraordinary attention on the cubs, I let them gradually learn that through my hands they would receive an endless diet of food, information, and affection. I made it a practice to *hand* them their rations. With my fingers I pointed out berries, grubs, salamanders, and roots. I was the hand that removed their ticks and stickers, lifted them over deadfalls, scratched their backs, and patted their heads.

If nature cheated porcupines, turtles, and armadillos out of any ability to get cuddly, she made up for the deficiency when she created bears. My personal enjoyment of a lapful of cubs every night was no greater than that of the cubs themselves. Their first nine days of fear and distance quickly gave way to a passionate urgency to press physically close and to have my fingers run constantly through their luxuriant fur when they sat with me on the big willow-bough and moose-thong chair.

That same night when they first climbed into my lap, they crawled into the roomy down sleeping bag with me. I liked their clean, fresh-straw smell, and their warm little bodies almost compensated for their snoring and abundance of voracious parasites.

After breakfast the next morning we had our first argument when I used Red Fern's can of flea and louse powder.

While I operated the sluice box that morning, shoveling tons of settlings into the trough and flooding the tailings, the bears wrestled or just sat on the crest of the bank above the creek and stared across the lake. Sometimes they ventured to the edge of the dusky forest until a blue jay or a whisky-jack chased them back to the placer box. During one period of excitement while I was concentrating on a handful of large nuggets that suddenly appeared at the same time, the cubs vanished. After climbing the bank to look for them, I discovered the trio raiding the blueberry and raspberry patch behind the smoke shed. Upon seeing me, they waddled their tightly packed little bellies across the clearing and slowly collapsed upon my boots. They had forgiven—indeed forgotten—the defleaing bee with which the morning began.

My day in the mud, spray, wind, insects, and rushing current had almost ended when a teeming run of sockeye salmon swarmed out of the lake and headed for spawning pools up Nugget Creek. Rushing to the tool shed where I kept fishing tackle, I seized appropriate gear and returned to the stream. An hour later I hung forty pounds of red salmon filets in the smoker. Dusty and Scratch ate half a gallon of roe and guts; but Rusty turned up his nose at the delicacy.

Had I known more about bears, I would have recognized a conspicuous symptom of illness when a cub refused salmon roe. I supposed Rusty to be gorged on berries. When he gazed up at me with a genuinely distressed expression and doleful whine, I picked him up, took him inside, and put him to bed. Sensing a crisis, Dusty and Scratch sat meekly together on the carpet. By nine o'clock that night, Rusty's condition had grown alarming. His little body was limp and without reaction when I touched him. His eyes were glassy, his mouth became dry and hung open, his breathing was explosive and irregular. Once he struggled to get up, but fell back in helpless resignation. I postponed despair by keeping a kettle of water boiling and by applying one hot towel after another against his abdomen until midnight. Then he vomited. What I saw made me fear I would have but two cubs come morning. He had eaten a quantity of lethal Amanita death-cap mushrooms, about which little bears' mothers are supposed to warn them. At three o'clock Dusty and Scratch slowly climbed up on the bed and nestled near Rusty, who didn't move or open his eyes. I kept the fire stoked until morning and wiped away the white froth as it oozed from his throat.

When the orange bands of dawn had widened into day, I thought I recognized a slight change for the better. Instead of the awkwardly helpless sprawl between Dusty and Scratch, he now reclined on his belly, legs folded neatly and purposely. His head pointed straight forward with his chin upon the edge of my pillow. But his eyes were still glazed and he couldn't open them more than halfway. When he finally fell into deep sleep with regular breathing, I decided to prepare breakfast. Dusty and Scratch followed me into the kitchen but slunk into a corner and sat like a pair of stuffed doorstops while I boiled a pot of oatmeal. They hadn't issued a sound since Rusty got sick. Instead of scrambling into the sun-flooded woods near the lake for their morning romp after breakfast as was their habit, the two silent cubs eased to their positions on the bed, one on either side of Rusty. Dusty licked his face for half an hour.

At noon Rusty made a painful effort to get off the bed. When I lowered him to the floor, he staggered to his bowl in the kitchen and drank nearly a quart of water. After declining offers of several kinds of food, he tottered outside for an attack of diarrhea. Upon returning inside, his woebegone expression indicated a desire to be lifted back onto the bed. By midafternoon the filmiest hint of sparkle returned to those bright little eyes that began to follow my movements as I cleaned the cabin. In a moment of exaltation, I scooped him up under my arm and insisted upon a mile walk down the brilliant beach.

"You damned little varmint," I whispered as I placed him on the sand, "you made me forget all about that hundred dollars' worth of nuggets I found yesterday!"

At first he waddled with stiff, sore insides, stumbling to the water's edge every few steps for a drink; but the enthusiastic antics of Dusty and Scratch barely in front of his nose eventually brought back some of that wild joie de vivre that characterizes bear youngsters, and at length he recovered most of his bouncing lope. By way of celebrating his recovery, I broke regimen by allowing him the luxury of chasing a raucous curlew across a boggy moor.

2

Danger Signals

Each day the cubs assumed greater importance to me.
As that importance grew, I became more determined
to school them in self-sufficiency. From the standpoint
of pure practicality, no sluice-and-pan mucklark with
college ahead could ever permanently satisfy the
appetites of three wild bears. Out of fairness to the
bears—and at least partly to repay the trust the old
she-bear had placed in me—I decided to forego morning
panning in favor of walking the cubs over a regular
course or forage range and teaching them to catch
grubs, meadow mice, voles, and lemmings by turning
stones, ripping the bark from deadfalls, and lifting
the ubiquitous mantle of sphagnum moss. I dipped their
paws into black wood ants' hills, bringing to the surface
swarms of delicious big juicy ants carrying their eggs.
At first the cubs were leery of the prissy army ants
that paraded up and down the beach, during the heat
of the day, with bits of leaves as parasols; but once
curiosity had led them to sample the insects, the bears
never failed to follow the long, two-way files of ants,
scooping them up with their tongues and spitting out
the leafy parasols.

About half a mile down the shore of Babine Lake
was a bog where the cubs dug through acres of marsh
grass for iris rhizomes and globe and sego lily bulbs.
In mid-July the strawberries and gooseberries became
sugary ripe, while chicory root, cress, and crocus pods
went a long way toward filling the cubs' expanding
stomachs. By August, our range cut a circular swath
five miles in circumference.

As cubs, Rusty, Dusty, and Scratch were the most observably happy-hearted creatures I have ever known. After those first few days of meekness and panic following their tragic abandonment, they faced new experiences every day with remarkable adaptability, vigor, and enthusiasm. I know they never forgot their mother during that first summer, because there were lapses into moody reflection during which they shinnied up the big fir, peered longingly up and down the lake, and cried softly—a ritual nothing could break up until the mood changed. They seemed to sense that something enormously important in their lives had come to an end. After the food walk each morning, they spent the afternoon near the sluice box, somersaulting in the reeds, catapulting down the slippery creek bank, wrestling, sparring, swimming, and gulping minnows, polliwogs, young frogs, and beetles.

One afternoon Rusty, who was always first to accept adventure, cornered a water snake about two feet long and swallowed it. After an analytic moment, he realized something was wrong. He stood erect on his hind legs, walled his big eyes, which seemed about to pop from his head, pounded his stomach, then regurgitated the wriggling, snapping snake. Dusty and Scratch looked on in horrified amazement as the serpent thrashed about at water's edge and finally swam away. After that experience, I never saw the cubs notice another snake. I soon learned, however, that regurgitation was about as normal for them as a bowel movement.

For all their playfulness, those cubs were very serious bathers. They seemed to realize that no parasite could survive submersion for long. Ticks, fleas, lice, chiggers, and no-seeums would let go and surface after five minutes under water. Since the flea-powder treatment disagreed with the cubs, we substituted for it a plunge in the lake every summer afternoon. After their bath, they would swim up the mouth of slow-moving Nugget Creek, climb into the sluice box where I was working, and as a practical joke, deliberately shower me as they shook the water from their fur. They swam almost exclusively with their forelegs, using a longer stroke than a dog.

For practical reasons I had taught the cubs their names. While weaning them from my dwindling supply of milk and cereal, I placed their dinner bowls on the edge of the kitchen counter. Out of the twisting, squirming, howling melee at my feet, I would call Scratch. Though at first he paid no attention, he soon learned to answer the call and receive his bowl. Dusty was always second, rather to Rusty's chagrin. Being the leader, he thought he should be first in everything, including eating. He had already learned his name from my calling him when salamanders floated into the sluice box. In order to avoid confusion between the two similar names, I trilled the "R" in Rusty. Even when engaged in rough-and-tumble games, each bear learned to come to me when I called him by name, but the other two would generally come also as if to make sure I was not playing favorites. The real test of response to their names, however, was calling them down from a tree in a different order each time. Uncannily, regardless of how I changed that order, no confusion ever resulted.

At seven months, assuming the cubs were born in January, their senses of smell, sight, and hearing were acutely developed. One morning when we were foraging a hillside for spicy fern fiddlenecks, all three cubs suddenly raced to me, tearing my clothes and scratching my legs, back, and arms until they bled, in a mad scramble to get aboard my shoulders. Like most action in the wilderness, this emergency came with surprising swiftness. The painful clawing, the moving furry weight upon my neck, the noise and the shock, slowed my reaction time. Under many conditions this might mean the difference between life and death. I have since observed that the apparent nonchalance of a slowly shuffling mother bear conceals an internal hair-trigger.

From their precarious perch, the snorting cubs glared intently in the direction of an aspen thicket. Within moments a mature boar bear rushed out, bellowing his disapproval of our invasion of his forage range.

Balancing myself against an alpenstock under the weight of the three squirming youngsters, all jockeying for top position on my head and shoulders, I tried to remind myself that zoologists had declared there was nothing dangerous about an untantalized bear, that bears were psychologically the nearest wild animal to man, and that a male bear would decamp at the smell of cubs, expecting fearful reprisals from their dam. The theory that adult bears are notoriously nearsighted must also have been partially proven, for when he suddenly got a whiff of us, the boar churned up a frightful roar, turned, and fled over the hill.

Rather than undergo a second clawing when the cubs began to slide back to earth, I lay down on the heath to facilitate their descent.

"Scoot, you little renegades!" I ordered.

I didn't purposely avoid all risky situations, but for days after the confrontation with the big bear, I fretted over the importance of the cubs' learning basic danger commands in order to tree instantly when we met deadly enemies. (Besides, though claw scratches heal, shredded trousers and shirts were too difficult to mend in the north woods.) Reflecting that timber wolves, lynx, wolverines, cougars, bull moose, and elk had better eyesight than boar bears, I spent many hours experimenting to try to find methods a mother bear might employ to order her brood up a tree, and, the danger past, to call them back to earth. Even though I never came up with the exact answer, as luck would have it one morning I chanced upon an effective substitute. We were walking that first section of our course, which led along the lakeshore, when a cow moose with twin calves stepped from a small ravine directly in front of us. The cubs' first closeup brush with a mountainous moose was terrifying. They stampeded to my legs for another climb to my shoulders. Dropping my walking stick, I clapped my hands in their faces and yelled, "Tree!" Demonstrating their own native acumen, Rusty and Dusty reacted spontaneously. The clap of my hands and the command "Tree!" ever afterward was their signal to shinny up the tallest available conifer in the fewest seconds. When the moose had passed, I brought them down by calling their names. It was as simple as that.

It didn't pass my observation, however, that Scratch was last up the tree. He had shrieked for me to pick him up before following his brother and sister to safety. On the following morning we were lifting the roofs of vole tunnels in a brome and millet meadow. With menacing booming and hissing, a pair of adult badgers popped out of a moss-concealed ambush and began to close the distance between themselves and the scattering cubs.

"Tree!" I shouted, at the same time clapping my hands, when the bears had almost reached timber. Rusty and Dusty made it; but at the command, Scratch turned and ran toward me. Both badgers took a shortcut, sprang at the timorous cub's throat, and were rapidly strangling him when I arrived with the sturdy alpenstock. Instead of obeying an inclination to cuddle the cub and dress his bleeding wounds after clobbering the badgers away, I clapped my hands and sternly shouted in his face: "Tree!" Even after he had joined Rusty and Dusty, the little fellow sobbed from a lofty limb for my sympathy. Although markedly slower to learn, Scratch was to demonstrate later that he was also slower to forget.

Despite their native endowments of instinct and intelligence, it was not an easy matter to teach them the self-sufficiency necessary for independent survival. They grew more and more anxious to please me—much more so, I thought, than the most slavishly inclined dog.

Rather than squelch any of that budding loyalty, I began to devise simple projects involving all four of us in situations of food hunting, sharing, defense, offense, and recreation. My goal was the maximum development of what was theirs to develop. Differentiating between what was natural for a bear and what was natural for man was often confusing to all of us. The results were admittedly dismal when it came to sharing one mouse or one mushroom; but when we discovered berry patches, or a group of four mushrooms, the cubs responded to my insistence on an equal division of the goodies. I forced myself to swallow that fourth raw mushroom in order to teach the point.

Taking full advantage of the cubs' cooperative attitude, I taught them selective listening in the presence of other sounds. When seesawing crickets, fiddling cicadas, pine sawyers, birds, bullfrogs, and squirrels were in highest-keyed cacophony, I purposely exposed the cubs to a hungry bitch coyote with long, empty teats and a velvet-pad approach, and to an arthritic old lynx with a limp, so as to sharpen even further their naturally keen sense of hearing. Both these predators were extremely dangerous due to their hunger, but slow. For both offense and defense, the ability to hear an important sound of far less intensity amidst louder but unimportant noises had to be learned early. Rusty and Dusty caught on very fast, but Scratch often tried my patience and that of the other two bears.

Left to themselves—as were their lot while I grubbed an ounce or so of gold pinheads from pan and sluice—they squandered their time plotting poker-faced mischief against one another, ricocheting from stump to stump, rolling down the bluff as one ball of snarling fur, and yelping and coughing their grievances from the top of the cliff. They tried to implicate me, as they had formerly implicated their mother, in both their fun and their disputes. As the weeks went by, it became increasingly difficult for me to remain on the sidelines when they teased me to join in their games.

I never harbored any notions of pampering those bears. Boiled down to hard reality, mothering was the part of cubhood they had to forego. My job was to "big brother" them into growing up. In the discharge of that duty, I tried as far as possible to enforce a mother bear's strict regimen of discipline, never tolerating one moment of disobedience, theft, or insolence. No mother bear would ever put up with bad behavior from a cub, and I never excused deliberate orneriness. I allowed them unrestrained joy when joy was well-defined in healthy play. But I

became cautious in the extreme, and, according to
the Indians, stricter than any mother bear.

No human could hope to equal a mother bear when
it comes to the amount of affection she lavishes upon
her young. She settles their arguments with kisses and
soft "vocabulary," she transports them piggy-back into
the fool's paradise of beardom where they all laugh,
play, eat, drink, and to heck with tomorrow. The fact
that the cubs were able to adapt themselves to my
rigid world was far more remarkable than any adjust-
ment I had to make.

On several exasperating occasions I heartily sub-
scribed to the late William T. Hornaday's counsel:
"If thine enemy offend thee, present him with a black
bear cub!" I recall from lengthy diary observations
a setting pine-grouse hen that Rusty and Dusty nosed
off her nest in one of the subtundra meadows north
of Nugget Creek. The incident occurred so swiftly
a hundred yards ahead of me that I was unable to
avert disaster. The two cubs, accustomed to crunching
and gulping frogs, mice, lemmings, and voles, had
never made a kill as large as a grouse. While they
chased the unfortunate bird and ripped out mouthfuls
of plumage, Scratch moved onto the nest and devoured
six eggs. In order to prolong the excitement, Rusty
and Dusty continued to pull feathers and bat the
screaming fowl back and forth between them until
the naked bird died, whereupon the two cubs engaged
in the first serious fight of their lives over the carcass.
More as a lesson than as a punishment, I confiscated
the dead grouse and stuffed it into a badger's den.
At such times I cursed my responsibility.

On one especially profitable afternoon, I became
so engrossed in the placer operation that I failed to
observe my three mischievous loafers. I hadn't allowed
them to wander alone into the cattails north of Nugget
Creek because an old mallard friend of mine was sitting
on a clutch of nine eggs which were due to hatch
shortly. On this particular afternoon the duck suddenly
took to the air, circling around and around me as well
as the area of the nest, and proclaiming starkest
tragedy.

I have never become reconciled to nature's callousness in permitting other animals to rob birds' nests.

Sensitive to the slightest change in the barometer of my feelings upon subjects they could comprehend, Rusty, Dusty, and Scratch hid out that evening under the bed farthest from my chair. I hadn't scolded them for their crime. They simply inferred from my loud yells and desolated mood how I felt about it. There was no need for discussion. They hadn't committed intentional deceit other than to sneak across the creek into off-limits territory. It was a natural type of original sin that could hardly be overcome. Long after I had gone to bed that night, three little bandits crawled gingerly under the covers, whining softly for peace of mind. I am certain they expected punishment, because bears keenly resent both insult and injury to themselves. They generally punish their own offenders. Apparently those three expected appropriate measures to be taken whenever they crammed their paws into the wrong cookie jar.

After Rusty had shown Dusty and Scratch how delicious big black wood ants were, the three bears spent endless hours chasing and devouring every insect that crawled or flew. One amusing incident involved a hornets' nest. Dusty was by far the most observant and aggressive of the three, and when she found the nest hanging from the underside of an alder limb, she inveigled Scratch into climbing the tree (by pretending she could not reach it) and knocking the miniature condominium to the ground. Scratch generally displayed real talent for seeking out and finding trouble. He felled the nest on the third pass, but not before the infuriated occupants had stung him on the ears, nose, and bare bottoms of his feet. While he bawled in pain from the alder limb, Rusty and Dusty not only ate the remaining hornets, but chewed up and swallowed most of their paperwalled apartment house.

When I gave Scratch the horselaugh because of the ridiculous plight he had allowed himself to be maneuvered into, he forgot his injuries, descended, and came over to me with his brother and sister. They all growled seriously about the insult and shook their heads at my feet. I never laughed at a bear or ridiculed one in any way after that. I don't wish to convey the impression that bears don't "laugh," because I believe they do. Rusty, Dusty, and Scratch deliberately sought entertainment that was funny for man *and* beast. Every day saw some new reason to engage in hearty belly laughter—but *with* the cubs, not *at* them. They were inordinately sensitive to the difference.

During many of our leisure hours when we romped on the sandy beach of Babine Lake or rolled in boisterous roughhouse through the meadow on the shoulder of the hill behind the cabin, I was sorely tempted to teach those eager learners some of the tricks of circus bears. The little show-offs frequently walked on their front paws, turned somersaults, or crowhopped through what lively imaginations might interpret as wild flamenco dances.

Tame bears, of course, are the most eminently trainable of all animals: according to trainers, they are not only more amenable to training than simians, but are far more dependable—even more so than dogs—when it comes to long, complicated repertories of tricks. I marveled each day at how manageable the cubs really were. Their bad habits were few indeed, and easily broken. Since I saw no value in it for the bears, I withstood the temptation to teach them tricks.

By the end of July we had been nearly a month without rain. Edible mushrooms—agarics, boletus, puffballs, shaggy manes, and morels—normally profuse at that time of the year, were no longer to be found in the meadows or along decaying logs in the forest. Berries were still plentiful, but bulbs and rhizomes were increasingly difficult to dig as the duff, or surface debris, and soil dried out. The five-mile foraging range was not adequate to support three growing appetites. Birds had abandoned the area. We had to preempt more territory, which meant, of course, pirating the food supply of other animals, and thus upsetting the balance of the total forest community. As it seemed that the canyon of Nugget Creek was the area of greatest natural yield, we made our way one morning along its bank through dense stands of catclaw, devil's fist, thimbleberry vines, willows, and alders to the beaver dam somewhat more than a mile above the lake. Half a dozen beavers, harvesting young willow shoots, swam to the safety of an island lodge they had created near the center of the pond. Interpreting the move as a challenge, the cubs plunged in and swam to the island. The beavers failed to return, so the cubs decided it was more fun to chase big landlocked salmon around the pool. I was always impressed by the swiftness and amount of strength in the cubs' forearms. Within minutes each dripping bear sat in a shallow, devouring a red salmon.

I was preparing my own breakfast the next morning when a tumultuous commotion behind the cabin attracted my attention. As there was no rear door, I had to run through the living room, across the front porch, down the steps, and around the dwelling before I could discover who was attacking whom. With fisheyed stares, the cubs were screaming their indignation from the lowest branch of their favorite fir, while the largest, calmest beaver I have ever seen stood upright, balanced against his tail, whistling at the outraged cubs. He wasn't angry, for he exhibited neither teeth nor bristled ruff. When I approached, he merely turned my way without losing his balance, and champed his teeth. His message failed to bring any reaction from the cubs. Motionless, they peered down in temporary silence, anticipating a violent eviction of the unwelcome visitor.

Repeating several whistles to the cubs and clicking his teeth at me, the beaver finally went off down the trail toward Nugget Creek. When I walked slowly after him, he hissed fiercely and repeatedly slapped the ground with his tail warningly. Watching from the edge of the bank, we listened to his sharp fifing long after he had begun the slow journey up the creek to the pond where he was probably king. Only after an examination of the pool during the course of the morning did I realize the cause of the beaver's agitation. During the night the water level had dropped far below normal. We would be treated henceforth as hostile interlopers if we continued to poach on other animals' territories for the dwindling food supply.

Other signs were abundant everywhere that morning. Bog and meadow plants, in the habit of wilting during hot summer days, had failed to regain their freshness during the dewless night because a warm chinook wind had blown in and dried not only the atmosphere but hillside springs as well. During one lull when the chinook was still, a gray mist rose a foot or so above the surface of the lake and gradually crept ashore like a giant amoeba which engulfed the cattails where the mallard hen still quacked for her stolen eggs. The fog drifted up Nugget Creek as if tantalizing the thirsty forest.

That evening there was no dew along the lakeshore. Instead of their usual tenor arias, the frogs engaged in short baritone ditties that seemed to repeat "Jug o' rum! Jug o' rum!" The notes of the frogs were always in lower key in time of drought. As we sat very still on the stoop through the warm twilight and watched the hollow, starry vault of night enclose our lakeside home, I became conscious of the fact that we were sitting literally on the bottom of a river of dry air that was flowing northward—a river whose hot whirlpools often gulped drifts of dead leaves and lifted them to an invisible surface far overhead where they floated away. As there was almost no exposed earth in the north woods, it was a drought wind without dust.

The next morning I went to the mouth of the creek to fish out a fresh breakfast, but neither trout, squawfish, nor salmon—not even suckers—would strike, because of the suffocating atmospheric pressure. By now the water level of the creek was perilously low for the thousands of sockeye that had returned from the sea to spawn. In addition to the lack of rain, Nugget Creek was without glacier reserve on the eastern slopes of the lordly Babine Mountains, and the water table along the great subterranean granite strata was unseasonably low. Light snowpacks for four successive winters had broken capillary connection with substrata reservoirs, and even the deepest-rooted conifers appeared to be in trouble. Should the stream dry up completely, all the salmon eggs that had been deposited on the sandy bottoms of eddies would die. The beavers would be driven from the creek to the lake, and the lives of all the hundreds of miniature creatures who had their habitat in the water and along its banks would be thrown out of natural cycle for generations.

The frivolous cubs were never ones to worry seriously even about empty larders. Noting definite chapping on the backs of my hands and across the bridge of my nose, I called the bears to rub their claws, naked soles, and noses with bacon fat to prevent their cracking. They rolled and gurgled during the new game, partly because of the novelty, partly because they enjoyed licking away the strongly flavored grease.

Unable to find food on the dry meadows and subarctic tundra, frogs, mice, voles, and lemmings, as well as insect larvae, disappeared from every sector of our forage range. Roots and rhizomes grew tough and stringy. The cubs adapted themselves almost overnight to grazing like ungulates on the few remaining clumps of buffalo grass, spike-rush, cattail brome, and glyceria.

The longer the drought persisted the skimpier the natural food supply became, regardless of how far we walked or whose domain we invaded. Our grub locker no longer yielded a satisfying meal for *one* cub, not to mention *three*. Most other bears had left the region in favor of the moister Fraser River Valley, gambling hunger against high-power rifles. We foraged for clover, timothy, fescue, and sweet vernal among the rocky tussocks above the meadows; but the time was at hand when all grasses, too, began to dry up. New tastes could be acquired only when there existed something to taste.

Grazers—deer, elk, bighorn, and mountain goat— were first to migrate to more provident pasture east of the Ominecas. They were followed, as a matter of course, by their predator tagtails: wolves, coyotes, lynx, and cougars. One morning I received the fright of my life. Rusty and Dusty always heeled well or worked slightly ahead of me. They seemed to know every square foot of the range, which included lake-shore, streamside, bog, meadow, aspen savannah, forest, and a welter of wind-raked ridges. Scratch often lingered behind even after he realized that the edibles of a given area had been exhausted. He would wander on his own, daydreaming aimlessly, rolling stones or chasing a butterfly he knew he couldn't catch. On the morning mentioned, Rusty, Dusty and I were about to swing down from an aspen thicket near the brow of a hill south of the cabin in order to explore a wind-browned meadow, when suddenly I saw a twitch in the flattened ears of a crouched, bush-and-grass-concealed cougar that was stalking Scratch. The cub as usual was loitering forty yards behind. I knew it would be fatal to send Rusty and Dusty up a tree while I rescued the smallest bear. The big cat could climb better than the cubs. So, turning back to alert Scratch, herding the other two bears as fast as they would herd without knowing the reason for the rush, and shouting until I almost choked on my own panic, I altered our habitual route and we ran most of the way home.

I kept a leery eye on the arthritic old lynx that by this stage of the drought was circling the cabin every afternoon. The famished coyote that was dangerously bold because she was with pups, and desperately hungry, also had designs on the cubs. After our experience with the lion, I never again left the cabin without Red Fern's 30-30.

As the situation deteriorated, I encouraged the cubs to invent and use their own danger warnings, sounds, and signs I could imitate: the low growl, the short, repeated hiss, the erect position with arms low, palms facing forward (the bear's fighting stance), the bared teeth, the setter-pointer freeze. We gave up all forms of play while foraging. Every move was toward training.

My own sensitivity to assorted snarls, snorts, and

raised upper lips was expanded to include an investigation of every erect position of hackles (one of the quickest ways to interpret a bear's mood). I watched especially for forefeet signals for attention such as pawing the ground, thumping the earth or a tree, a hasty move toward timber. The cubs had learned a reassuring alertness.

Thus, after such intensive training, it was not unreasonable to assume that Rusty had an urgent message about seven o'clock one August morning. I was in the kitchen up to my elbows in dirty pots and pans when the cub rushed into the cabin, stood up, thumped a cupboard door for attention, and gargled incomprehensibly. He indicated by pulling my pants leg with his teeth that I should drop what I was doing and follow him. Never knowing what to expect from those little Katzenjammers, I always investigated their signals.

The atmosphere, even at that early hour, seemed separate and apart from the breathy heat. When we reached the clearing at the rear of the cabin, a puff of dry southwest chinook slapped my face with ashy haze. The blast bore the pungent, terrifying odor of pine smoke. Rusty's message was clear. Somewhere along a not too distant watershed above the headwaters of Nugget Creek, the forest was on fire.

3

Forest Fire

In these parched days, there was no longer enough water flowing in Nugget Creek to operate the sluice trough. Refugee trout were migrating down to the lake as fast as they could wriggle, half-exposed, through the shallows, but salmon were dying before they could lay and fertilize their eggs. Tracks and fish skeletons along the banks and beaches indicated the remaining bears, racoons, foxes, martens, minks, and otters. Weasels, too, were feasting upon the fishy windfall. Rusty, Dusty, and Scratch had grown tired of stale, raw salmon. I boiled the most recently deceased with wild onions, parsnips, chicory root, dandelion root, and mustard stalks to concoct a sort of muskeg bouillabaisse that for several days at least would stay the cubs' growling intestines should the fire compound the threat of famine with that of destruction.

The lake water just beyond the half-bare mouth of the creek was alive with sockeye salmon whose run upstream was far behind schedule. They would not be able to make it, and thus subsequent generations of the lively game fish, like the defeated trout, would certainly feel the pinch.

Mile-high thunderheads over the eastern slopes of the Babine Range and the big awkward hills south of Mount Netalzul were jabbing frightfully hot bolts of lightning into the cavernous gloom of the tinderbox forest. The fire front glowed along the edges of the Chapman Lake country twenty miles southwest of Babine Lake. The smoke cantered our way on the back of the panting chinook. A shroud of flaky, white ashes began to cover the ground and filter into the cabin. I could only pray that those massive thunderheads meant rain which would extinguish the blaze and put an end to the dangerous thirst. Every two hours we climbed the hill for a look into the smoke-filled valley which cradles Chapman Lake.

Like a whole chord on a piano as opposed to its component notes, the total smell of a forest fire is distinct from that of individual combustibles within the timberland. Smells of pine pitch, green leaves, duff, and wood emerge as a soggy odor of rotten mushrooms and burnt rags completely unlike the wonderful fragrance one might expect from a woodland fireplace.

More to pass the time than hoping for effective results, I cut all brush and dry herbage around the cabin and burned it along the duff which I raked from the forest floor. I carried water, five gallons at a time, from dying Nugget Creek and filled the rain barrels against the time when sparks might ignite the split shake roof of the cabin.

By noon the following day the creek no longer ran. All thunderheads had evaporated after their lightning had set a new arc of fires. Unless the wind changed, we were now in the direct path of the main holocaust which was but ten miles away, leveling centuries of woodland production to smoldering ash at the rate of two miles per hour along a fifteen-mile front, suffocating and cremating every living creature within its devastating swath. When the nearest perimeter of the fire crept to within five miles of the cabin, I tied my canoe alongside Red Fern's landing and packed all our indispensables, including my friend's personal effects which I considered valuable to him. The chinook subsided temporarily, granting extra time to cover the roof with wet sand while the fire was still three miles away. The clouds of blue-gray smoke now billowed straight up instead of belching horizontally into our faces. Although the cubs were restless, climbing one tree after another, burrowing beneath the cabin floor, and all the while snarling and cuffing one another, they exhibited perhaps less resignation than I did. After preparing and loading the canoe, I spent most of the afternoon hauling buckets of sand which I spread over the roof.

Suddenly I remembered. There were three families of nestlings in the path of the fire. I dropped the sand bucket and herded the cubs into the cabin.

Since the incidents with the grouse and duck nests, I had keenly scrutinized every bush and meadow for occupied bird nests the length and breadth of the cubs' range. Most species were on the wing by the middle of August, but late migrators were still nesting. In the dry grass at the far edge of the upper meadow was a nest of horned larks. Four pinfeathered robins too young to fly were still in a nest on the cottonwood branch near the beaver pond. A family of hermit thrushes in a gooseberry clump near the crest of the hill south of the cabin were even more helpless.

After locking the cubs inside the cabin, I grabbed

a cardboard carton from the tool shed and raced off toward a distant ridge where flames were leaping from treetop to treetop. It was a long, rough two miles at the end of a difficult day. There was no trail much of the way.

When I could see the gooseberry clump, it was on fire. The parent thrushes had called until their voices were no longer natural, but I could still hear them above the cackling, cannonading roar of the advancing wall of orange flame. The intense heat began to sear my face and hands. My clothes were so hot I feared they might burst into flame at any moment. Salty perspiration coursed through my eyes and into my mouth. I had arrived five minutes too late. Like the parents, I was forced to retreat and watch a flaming branch crash with an explosion of sparks into the burning gooseberry bush.

A mile to the northwest, along the shoulder of the same ridge, was the upper meadow where the horned larks were raising quadruplets. As I plunged along, only partially avoiding catclaw and berry vines, I wondered what kind of mischief the cubs were inventing back at the cabin. When I reached the meadow and knelt into the deep, dry grass, the two parent larks came and sat alongside each other on the rim of the nest as those foolish, friendly little birds were in the habit of doing. All six members of the family stared up at me through smoke-teared eyes. They were not afraid.

The fire was closing in. Time or contemplation had run out. I had to make the decision and act within a matter of moments. The meadow was a hundred yards wide and half a mile long, with open gravel over which the flames would not leap, but the birds would surely perish where the brushy forest stood within ten feet of the next. The grass was like dry excelsior. In a moment of sheer rashness, I picked up the nest and rushed it to the center of the meadow where I concealed it in another clump of grass. The parents followed. When I left, they were both singing softly to the nestlings. If they could but survive heat and smoke, they would all live. It was a chance I had to take.

At the beaver pond the emergency was even more acute. Although the canyon hardwood forest of cottonwoods, willows, alders, dogwoods, and the understory of broadleafed herbs and shrubs burned much more slowly than the resinous softwood conifers of the open hillsides, the gorge furnished the flames a continuous up-draught of oxygen like a fireplace with a chimney. The main fire front was creeping slowly down both sides of the ravine of Nugget Creek toward Babine Lake.

The parent robin hen lay dead at the foot of the cottonwood directly beneath her nest, apparently a victim of smoke inhalation. The cock had either fled or died somewhere. I jumped, grabbed the end of the branch, pulled it down, removed the next with the four groggy nestlings in it, and placed it inside the cardboard carton. The flames in the tops of the trees were about to exhaust the canyon of its oxygen and suffocate all life beneath. I began to feel weak and to lose the desire to get back to the cabin.

Slogging my way down the muddy creek bed through rotting fish remains, I suddenly realized that the blaze was now less than a mile from the cabin. Should the dwelling ignite or should smoke, heat, and lack of oxygen render our position untenable, I should have to take the cubs and my newest acquisitions into the canoe and cross the lake for the night. Since darkness at that time of year did not settle completely over northern British Columbia before ten o'clock, there still remained two full hours in which to feed bears and birds and try to arrive at the most reasonable immediate conclusions.

The worried faces of Rusty, Dusty, and Scratch were lined up at the front windowpane inside the cabin when I stepped to the porch. They coughed and wheezed an ecstatic greeting as if I had been gone a week. It was the first time I had ever locked them up or left them alone. Their rolling, tumbling, joyful display showed both relief and affection, like that of a dog when his master returns home. I was thankful that they had been too terrorized to wreck the inside of the cabin or swat at their images in the glass windows. They were momentarily nonplussed and peeved at the rudeness I used to make clear to them that the robins were neither to be eaten nor fooled with. I did not let the cubs go outside right away, because the beavers were arriving from their pond. More fortunate by habit and physical construction than their neighbors when an entire animal community faced a forest fire, the colony simply hiked the mile and a quarter to the lake, where as aquatics they were well adapted to survive.

Rarely inclined to act seriously, the cubs always recognized seriousness in me and respected, outwardly at least, my three nonnegotiable edicts:

Thou shalt not eat certain mushrooms;

Thou shalt not try to intimidate a moose, lynx, mountain lion, or grizzly;

Thou shalt not rob bird nests.

After their initial romping, cuffing, and licking my hands, Rusty—most perceptive and responsible of the trio—indicated by pulling my trouser leg toward the door that I should be aware of what was happening down on the beach. Placing the carton containing the nest on a cub-proof shelf above the fireplace, I accompanied the bears to the edge of the bluff overlooking the beach. There before us was probably the most distressing sight in all nature. Along the lakeshore, as far north and south of Nugget Creek as I could see, stampeded the horde of refugees the fire had scourged before it—those who for some reason had refused to migrate even though the duration of the drought had pointed with reasonable certainty to the imminent holocaust. Now, predators and prey ran side by side in horrified confusion. Fawn passed lion without recognition from either. Hare and lynx, moose calf and wolf trotted back and forth in search of lost families and further escape from a common enemy against which there could be no defense. The old female coyote with the sagging teats crawled up to the steps alone, singed and blistered, with deep burns along her back as if some falling torch had pinned her to the ground. By the hopelessness of her blank expression, I felt her cubs must be dead. I killed her with the 30-30.

The heat generated during the destruction of the forest behind the cabin became so intense and the air so unbreathable that I decided to take the robins and the bears to the opposite shore of the lake without further delay. As I was placing the cubs into the canoe between the fore thwart and the bow wedge, a mule deer doe limped to the beach from the coulee of Nugget Creek. Her back still smoking from the ordeal she had just undergone, she stumbled and fell into shallow water ten feet from the canoe. Beyond any hope of recovery from extensive burns and leg wounds, she watched with wide-set, soft-brown eyes and pleaded with hoarse bleatings as I levered a cartridge into the chamber of the rifle and did what I had to do. If the swarming throng of bewildered animals up and down the beach recognized the report of the gun, there was no outward sign.

As the heat from the fire increased, deer, elk, moose, and one grizzly bear plunged into the lake and began to swim toward the eastern shore. Farther out on the water dark forms bobbed like corks in the early twilight as other desperate creatures labored for life and safety. Keeping a sharp look for the exhausted as I paddled, I was able to overtake and pick from the pallid, mercury-like surface a red squirrel, two fawns, and a wolf cub. When I brought the growling wolf aboard, one of the awkward fawns became so frightened it fell over the gunwale and drowned before I could turn the canoe around and reach him. After releasing the weary refugees, who were strangely loathe to leave the security of the boat once we reached the eastern shore, I buried the carton with the young robins under a cairn of heavy cobble. The canoe unloaded, I relaunched for another trip in search of discouraged swimmers. The strangest rescue was that of a full-grown, white-haired porcupine. He swam eagerly up to the canoe but was unable to claw his way up the slick hull to the gunwale. Afraid to slip a hand under the swimming cactus, I offered him the blade of the paddle, which he grabbed and held with four feet and teeth until I could lift his thirty-five pounds into the hull of the canoe. Rusty, Dusty, and Scratch huddled under the seat next to my legs, sniffing, snarling, and growling at the silent ball of quills and stiff hair amidships.

When we had brought aboard two squirrels, one racoon, and a white-spotted woodland caribou calf—all too exhausted even to raise their heads from the bottom of the canoe where I had plopped them—darkness forced us to return to the eastern shore. It was surprising how seven of the eight animals aboard ignored me and the rippling of the water past the gliding craft. They all lay perfectly still and stared at the shivering, vomiting porcupine. Once ashore, they reacted like the first group, reluctant to disembark; in fact, I allowed the boycotted porcupine to remain all night in the beached canoe.

Across the lake the massive forest fire glowed reddish-orange and stabbed its miles of quivering fangs into the smoky sky—a phenomenon of terrible beauty and irresistible fascination despite the knowledge of countless individual tragedies, within its inferno. For an hour the cubs and I sat on the gravel beach silently contemplating the flickering skyline and grotesquely sprawling reflections upon the lake. As a result of what I saw that day, I was certain that no animal shared the pagan human pyrolatry or fire worship that may still be latent in varying degrees in each of us even after we've seen nature's young incinerated in their cradles.

Despite my lack of appetite, I prepared a huge pot of oatmeal for the cubs, whom not even a forest fire could distract from the sacrament of a meal. The night was a poor one for rest. I spread out the sleeping bag and lay down with the cubs, but memories of the horrors of that day became so magnified within my mind—as things always do at night—that I thought I was cracking up.

As individuals succeeded in crossing the lake, they would call until their throats were raw for mates and offspring, or would shriek from the pain of burns once out of the anaesthetizing cold of the water. By 3:00 A.M. the smoke dropped to the surface of the lake and piled up along the eastern shore, where we coughed and sneezed until dawn. White, floury ashes blanketed the landscape like a thin layer of snow.

I attributed the absence of a sunrise to the heavy stratum of smoke, through which I could no longer trace the progress of the fire, but when it was light enough to see, I realized the sky was also overcast with thick, dark nimbus. The first gentle rain soon extinguished the last ember within the skeleton forest and washed the atmosphere clean of the last traces of suffocating smoke.

While I was repacking the canoe in order to get back to Red Fern's cabin before a downpour—if indeed a cabin still existed—I witnessed the double tragedy inherent in every forest fire. Predators native to the eastern shore of Babine Lake stood by with gleaming eyes to reap a harvest of the weary, confused, and lost who had reached the shore after the debilitating swim. I watched a buck mule deer struggle up to the base of a cliff where he turned and faced three timber wolves. The deer was so fatigued he had to spread his legs wide apart in order to remain standing. In this cornered position, with his rump flattened against the cliff, he could still rip a wolf wide open with his lowered antlers. They weren't about to charge, though they fenced close to the deer's head and took turns lunging to wear the buck down. Before I could interfere, the deer turned his head to scare a fly from his flank. The unguarded second was all the wolves needed to spring simultaneously at the victim's throat.

A further manifestation of the effects of the fire that morning lay in the multitude of floating dead, from the tiniest shrews to elk and caribou—killed by fatigue, fear, burns, or drowning. The western shoreline near the cabin was a loathesome charnel pile of dead bodies, animals whose strength and will had been consumed in reaching the beach. When the refuge afforded by the lake had finally been achieved, they had been helpless to take advantage of it. I made no effort to restrain the cubs from collecting mice, packrats, squirrels, and chipmunks, all of which were strewn along the shoreline by the hundreds.

We found Red Fern's cabin undamaged.

To feed the orphan robins required far more time than I had calculated. Having been with Rusty, Dusty, and Scratch for six weeks, I was unaccustomed to guests who were finicky about their diet to the point of spitting out everything they disliked. Through experiment I found the robins were extravagantly fond of a concoction I whipped up from corn meal mush, powdered eggs, and pemmican. Of course the bears whiffed the expensive mixture as I prepared it. They raised boisterous cain when I reserved it exclusively for the birds.

On the rainy afternoon following the fire, after loading Red Fern's 30-30, I called the cubs for a walk through the silent, black, reeking skeleton of the forest to determine whether any wounded animals remained in some ravine or gully. In the ashen silence we found no tingle of life and breath and pulse. Even the smells were foreign to the living. Gone was every sound that makes up the mysterious hum of a living forest. Deadfalls and burned-out pockets of duff made walking exceedingly difficult.

When we reached the blackened meadow, I sent the bears back down the hill while I investigated the situation of the horned larks. The unfortunate family lay suffocated in the nest. The parent larks would have flown after me had I taken the little birds in the carton. For those few moments it had been within my province, blind and panicky, to unite the family other than in death.

Returning to the cabin by way of the muddy, fire-gutted Nugget Creek ravine, I determined to depart for Topley Landing as soon as the storm blew over. There was no further reason to remain. The creek might not flow again before the following spring. The cubs could not possibly forage in the gaunt desert of charcoal and ashes; my own food supplies were uncomfortably low.

I was surprised to hear several outboard motors

on the lake while I was preparing supper. Through my binoculars I saw parties of Indians in Hudson Bay bateaux who were arriving from Topley Landing to salvage venison for jerky and hides for leather from the bloating flotsam. The first boatload of Sekanis docked at Red Fern's landing to inquire about my welfare. They relayed the message to other families, all of whom began to laugh and sing as they worked in the rain.

Under the conditions of squally weather and shifting winds that followed, I dared not launch a whimsically inclined canoe into the uncertainties of fifty-five miles of open lake where capricious northern weather always wears a grotesque mask to defy and even hoodwink anyone who ventures to predict what it will do. It required no great effort of imagination to picture the bleakness of my chances of quickly approaching Topley Landing, especially since the hazards of the climate were compounded by four robins calling incessantly for their parents and three bear cubs whose overworked sense of humor included deliberate rocking of the boat.

4

Personae Non Gratae

Within a week the beach was clean, fragrant—almost alive once more. The carrion had been eaten or dragged away by transient scavengers. The cubs had eaten their share. Rain and wind has dissipated most of the smells of death and burning. Only the stark, blackened miles of ashy devastation remained to haunt the memory of that once luxuriant singing wilderness.

To get away from the desolation and the hollow sounds of the wind as it swept down to the lake, I decided to paddle across and move along the unburned eastern shore in the general direction of Topley Landing. When I reached the halfway point, it became evident that this side exposed me to an even more panoramic view of the burned-over areas. So I crossed back and followed within twenty feet of the western shoreline. Avoiding any shortcuts across the mouths of bays and inlets, I could now see less of the effects of the catastrophe, owing to the clifflike banks that rose some fifty feet back from the beaches. Still I could not escape the six-foot-wide band of floating bits of charcoal that rode the ripples at the water's edge and covered the once clear white sand. The recent rain, running off the denuded hills, had floated these vast quantities of charcoal into the lake.

Within fifteen miles, the mysterious and seemingly senseless waste from the fire thinned out where a new forest was winning its way back into an area that had been burned many years before. The fire had not attacked the new growth. I wondered if the bears shared my joy when the shore changed to a clear beach of rippled sand rising to a low crest covered with brome and saxifrage. The cubs, too, seemed to show more interest now and attentively watched the new forest.

During those first fifteen miles we saw very few animals. The only song to reach our ears was the wind's doleful interpretation of its new freedom as it whistled through the black silhouettes that leaned against one another at unnatural angles on the hills above the lake. The sound recalled childhood outings at Oso Flaco in California where my brother Sam and I used to romp among the Pacific dunes and listen to the tumult of the wind and waves amid the great oaken ribs of the wrecked schooner *Stella del Norte*. The words of my little brother echoed as clearly in my memory as if he had spoken them only a moment before, rather than long years ago: "The wind's a-coolin' 'er broilin' ribs so's the waves can gnaw 'er bones!"

Rusty, whose place in the pecking order was firmly established, occupied the bow wedge, licking his chops and staring ahead like a pirate navigator. Dusty and Scratch quarreled and cuffed each other over the starboard position on the forward seat, which offered the closest view of lakeshore activity. When they tried to sit next to me on the stern seat, they interfered with my paddling, so I had to chase them forward.

The calling of horned larks was the first animal sound to return. I'm sure the feelings of the bears were quite different from mine as they cocked their ears to listen to these wonderful songs, which reminded me only of my poor judgment.

Here and there we passed singed and wounded animals that had limped beyond the ruins of their former ranges and were now competing with healthy animals and inevitably losing in the struggle for food and living space. When a healthy fox, deer, or coyote studied us from the beach, the cubs would pound the gunwale and snarl or whine. The robin nestlings in the carton under the stern seat chirped their displeasure with both the darkness and their incarceration, but distasteful as a cage of any kind might be either to me or to the birds, that had to be their lot for yet a while. They peeped excitedly and nibbled my fingers when I reached from time to time into the box to assure them that they had not been abandoned. The bears, accepting my authority in a sort of filial cooperation, disdained the robins with scornful side glances and were plainly jealous when I stopped every two hours to feed the birds. The cubs' accusing eyes were far more eloquent than any words they might have used had they been endowed with the gift of speech.

At about three o'clock that first afternoon on the lake, the headwind became too strong for one man in a heavily loaded canoe to face, so I began to look for a campsite. I was only mildly concerned about the cubs, because they hadn't sauntered beyond touching distance the night we spent in the open on the eastern shore of the lake during the fire. I was gambling that they would not leave the hand that stroked, scratched, and fed them. Nor did predators worry me, for I knew the few that remained were still gorging themselves on easier prey among the wounded refugee population. At length I slipped into a protected little cove where a freshet trickled into the lake. There were low banks, a wide beach, and open forest palisades of spruce, fir, and hemlock, with alders and maples along the shallow arroyo of the creek. The site was practical, since I could walk the cubs from here to shelf-bogs above timberline on the hillside just south of the arroyo. The sparse natural forage included dry meadows and elderberry patches in which to graze. Although by now we were out of the burned area, there was no escape from the effects of the long drought. The trees and shrubs were green, but except for elderberries, the edible herbs and roots in the seepage bogs had been overgrazed by the nonmigrants. No matter how far we walked I could see no prospect of a well-rounded dinner for hungry cubs. Rainbows and Loch Levins were punching their heads through the surface of the lake near the mouth of the creek, as they always did for the cargo of exotic goodies that floated down from the hills, but they ignored every lure that concealed a fishhook.

In order to remove temptation from curious animal visitors, I hoisted my food supply over a heavy branch, out of reach from above or below. Once while canoeing down the Liard River in the Northwest Territories, I had made the mistake of tying my pack to a breakable branch. Two or more bears—whatever it took —climbed out on the limb, broke it off, than casually swiped all my staples.

After a long hike up the creek and back by way of a bald ridge of time-eroded scarps where edible lichens grew (rock tripe, lungworts, and caribou moss), we returned to camp. Having shared my last can of pork and beans, we relaxed on a log by the campfire to listen to the chorus of the pines. As the trees swayed, so the forest rippled in the waves of wind. Chirring grouse strutted down to the stream for a drink. Squirrels clamored from tree to tree, scolding and chattering as they tore pine cones apart for the nuts.

A single spider performed endless acrobatics on a webby trapeze directly overhead. I was smoking my pipe, trying to analyze the component sounds of evening. Rusty sniffed the breeze; Dusty lay on my lap with her head on my knee, facing the fire; Scratch sat turning a piece of bark, first with his right paw, then with his left.

Quite out of nowhere—as is usually the case—a full-grown black bear soft-padded up to the log. All three cubs watched her approach with the most disinterested regard, so I decided that rather than order them into a tree I'd watch what happened. There was no initial champing of teeth, no tense ripples of shoulder muscles, no hissing, no raising of hackles.

She was a rangy old girl who lifted her lips and grumbled a bit every time she looked my way. I was determined to keep up the bluff. As she paraded back and forth in front of me on her hind legs, she kept her forearms typically widespread with all ten four-inch claws facing outward and cocked for an uppercut should I commit an indiscretion. To the uninformed, this half-belligerent attitude of hers might have brought visions of her hugging a victim to death. The only existing adult bear hug is a horseplay technique carried over from cubhood. In addition to being harmless, the act is really an expression of friendship rather to be appreciated than dreaded. This old veteran with the rounded belly reeked of carrion, thus I realized her visit was social instead of piratical. She was deeply curious as to why the creature on the log whose species had always shot at her should suddenly appear fondling three of her kind.

As stated earlier, bears are among the wild animals psychologically closest to man. There are bright bears, dull ones, and a wide, bell-curve majority with normal "IQ's." This particular female would have had to be classed with the mentally retarded. After long hesitation she decided—temporarily—that I was harmless if approached no closer than six feet. I was delighted with her standoffishness. Another obvious index of her intelligence was her cautious fear of the cubs. After an eventual, bored investigation which consisted of stiff-legged circling and sniffing, frown-wrinkled brows, and gutteral mumblings, they returned to the log, Dusty to my lap, Rusty to my right side, and Scratch to my left. Still observing six feet of no-man's-land, the old bear sat down on the sand and leaned back against the same log. Turning her head from side to side, she studied the wriggling Scratch, who possessed the faculty of sitting acrobatically. I resumed my pipe while all five of us then reflected upon the dying embers of the campfire.

Suspended beneath the food pack and swaying in the softening evening breeze, the well-fed robins slept in their carton.

I was not surprised to find the old bear still in camp the following morning, but I was put out at the behavior of the cubs. Instead of leaving with her, as I must honestly confess I had faintly hoped for their sake they would, they snarled and snapped viciously at her heels. Finally driving her into the forest, they would not allow her to finish the smoked salmon I had given her for breakfast.

Despite pictographs and paintings found in caves and on cliffs depicting the struggle between ancient man and bears, nearly all Canadian Indians I have known considered bears an ancient race of people. They pointed to the bear's five toes on each foot, to his ability to walk and run on his hind legs, to the fact that all species possessed much the same traits, and to the dental cavities of those whose diets included too many sweets. Aside from certain simians, the bear is the only animal known to throw objects back and forth between two or more individuals. It couldn't have escaped even the most amateur observer that bears have another point in common with man in that they train their young in offense, defense, food procurement, and play.

Essentially true sons of the forest and open hillsides, bears—except the polar variety—are the only wild mammals without natural camouflage. Considered carnivores by most zoologists, they have an enviable digestive system that assimilates the widest variety of diet in the animal kingdom. Many people still believe the old cliché, "As nearsighted as a bear." Owing to the fact that its eyes are placed forward and close together on its face, a bear's vision is limited only as to angle, not distance. Some biologists feel that of all animals the bear is best adapted to Temperate Zone habitats.

The closer we approached the hamlet of Topley Landing the more Indians we saw: isolated families occupying cabins, fishing parties in bateaux, backwoods groups paddling piroguefuls of supplies toward remote and secret claims.

"I'll give you a dollar for one o' them cubs," offered one surly, obviously loaded Indian who pulled up alongside in a dinghy with an outboard. "How come they ain't chained?"

"What would you do with him?" I asked, laughing.

"Roast the little son-of-a-bitch, of course. Ain't you never et roasted cub? Better'n pork any day!"

Indians are the world's best readers of optical expression.

"So long!" I called when he was under way.

Early on the third morning we arrived at Topley Landing, and as luck would have it, the day turned out to be Sunday. Breakfast smoke carrying the fragrance of bacon, eggs, fresh bread, and trout from the shoreline row of silent, unpainted clapboard shacks still hung like a stratified mist barely above the glassy surface of the water. Nothing drives a bear to more insane gyrations than the smells of frying bacon and scrambled eggs. The cubs proved it. They whined, seesawed back and forth on their front, then on their hind paws, drooled and chewed the gunwales. Half a dozen little children giggled from the public jetty as we pulled in. One unobstructed look at the white man with three cubs sent them howling away to their homes. As the news spread, more yells, barks, and shouts between houses broke out to spoil some of the charm of the primitive village. Within moments the landing swarmed with dogs, fat squaws in calico or knitted dresses, men in blue denim shirts and jeans and widebrimmed black hats, and an assortment of hobbledehoys giggling between bursts of Babine dialect.

I kept enough distance to safely separate dogs and bears. Both were daring one another to get within chewing range.

"Is Red Fern in town?" It was a general question directed to anyone who might care to answer.

"Naw!" one man volunteered. "He's in the south, marking fell-trees for the Company."

"The South" could mean ten miles or five hundred.

"When will he be back?"

"Hard to say. Maybe today."

"Does he know his cabin didn't burn?"

"Yeah," the spokesman answered. "We've been up there collecting hides and jerky. How come you didn't suffocate?"

"Took the cubs and paddled across the lake till the rain put the fire out."

He translated for those less facile in English. Little full-moon faces began peering from behind the long pleated calico or knitted skirts of wide-bottomed squaws.

"Is the trading post open?" I asked.

"Not today. It's Sunday. Maybe Hank Morgan will open up before Mass. Lives behind the store. Priest gets here once a month. Supposed to be here today. Shows a movie to everybody that attends the service. Nobody wants to miss the show."

"What time is Mass?"

"Whenever the priest gets here. Roads are pretty bad since the rain. Look for him about noon. If he can't make it before tomorrow, he'll declare tomorrow Sunday."

"Any place I could lock up my bears till I can get outfitted?"

"Sure, in the stew pot. That's the only way we take to bears around here."

I got the impression it was white men, not bears, that were unwelcome for a reason I couldn't understand at the time.

"How far is Pendleton Bay?"

"Thirty-five, maybe forty mile. Nobody around here gonna hurt them bears."

"Could I pay a boy to paddle the canoe around while I go in and get my supplies?" I asked.

"I'll do it for fifty cents," one boy offered.

"I'll do it for a quid of t'bacca," said another.

"I'll do it for nothin'," several shouted, anxious to paddle on any terms a canoe with three live bears in it.

I picked a big, serious-looking boy named Barney and told him to get aboard when I pulled up alongside the dock. I wanted the bears to get acquainted with him before I left for the trading post. The nervous lad sat on the fore thwart behind the seat and stroked the bears, who whined and bristled but didn't snap. As I paddled farther out on the lake, the crowd dispersed and the noisy dogs trotted away. When we docked there was no one in sight except a few older men.

"Keep it about a hundred yards from shore, Barney. I'll get back as soon as I can."

"As you say in the States, no sweat!"

The boy sculled from the landing and paddled rapidly away before the cubs were totally aware of the maneuver. Once cognizant of my perfidy, however, they bawled their grievance with such force that six yelping mongrels returned to the jetty.

I was slopping along the muddy street toward the trading post when pandemonium broke out a hundred yards behind me. There, wallowing in the muck, was a howling melee of the six dogs in deadly grips with Rusty, Dusty, and Scratch. I ran back as fast as I could but not before a circle of Indian men had surrounded the fight. They would not allow me to rescue the bears.

"Tree! Tree! Tree!" I shouted at the top of my lungs, at the same time clapping my hands. Fortunately there was a tall pine at the edge of the quagmire. Three slippery little mudballs shot between the legs of the encircling natives before they could stop them. One man was toppled into the deep ooze, and others'

Sunday-go-to-meeting attire was splattered from head to foot. The unrecognizable bears gained safety and simulated innocence on the first branch of the pine while the muddy dogs yelped and jumped at the trunk in frustration. It was under these trying circumstances that I noted a different tone in each cub's voice. Ever so slight at the time, the differences of depth, timbre, and resonance were to assist me ever afterward in identifying each bear, especially at night, by the sound of his voice.

One irate Indian youth, whose bleeding hound had underestimated the cubs' sharp little claws and teeth, was headed for the tree with a .22. At the same time a pickup truck turned into the street from Topley Road. In an incredible stroke of luck, Clete Melville and Red Fern slid to a stop near the spot where the Indian and I were grappling over the rifle. At the sight of Melville, the Indians grabbed their dogs, the young man with the rifle got up and ran toward his home, and the crowd simply vanished.

"I rather expected you today," Red Fern said. "That's why I got Clete to bring me in. What's all the ruckus?"

Panting, I explained.

"There's several things here you wouldn't understand," said Melville. "Of all the animals, the Indian has greatest respect for a bear. It's not that he fears the animal; it's ancient folklore. If an Indian has to kill a bear under circumstances of direst necessity, he'll make some sacrifice, generally a whopper."

"They weren't inclined to call off their dogs just now," I reminded him. "That little bastard with the twenty-two was about to shoot the cubs."

"Yeah, they were hoping to liberate the bears' spirits. Those people weren't angry. They think the bear is superior to man and they object to your daring to associate with these cubs. In the Indian mind, you should never have taken the cubs after their mother was killed. They believe Gitchy Manitou would have looked after the bears by giving them another mother. It's been the only topic of conversation since Charley

Thwaite brought in the news. I'll get Morgan to open up his store so you can get your supplies. I suggest you leave here as soon as possible. These Indians may devise a way to kill those cubs.

"Another thing, we've got a squabble on our hands with all this talk about this lake country being made a national game refuge. Maybe even a park."

Clete Melville was the constable, an honest, sincere hulk of a middle-aged man whose physical strength and mental agility every Indian admired and respected. Many the chin of the unjust that had felt his pistonlike punch; many the underdog who had felt the lift of his powerful arms! Aside from his withering stare, no one ever forgot the slow cadence of his voice, which sounded as if it were coming up from a deep cellar. Clete was a self-tutored individual who often jousted with the sails of windmills. Some said he deserved his evil reputation as a lawman; others inferred that he had simply bypassed all the official lunacy of his office to enforce—even enact—the law as he saw it, letting the chips—and jawbones—fall where they would. He operated on the tenet that no one ever lived right in his own thinking and committed an outside evil.

"Never saw a man I wanted to imitate," he declared as we walked toward the trading post, " 'specially after I found out what's under his skin." He removed his slouch felt hat to run his fingers slowly through a thicket of unruly auburn hair.

There was nothing grotesque either in Melville's features or in his normal movements, but the Indians seemed to hunker into corners and doorways as we walked by. The deadpan expression from his hollow blue eyes caused me mentally to place two crossed femurs under his chin. I assumed the Indians cringed from the same image, one of terrifying loneliness and explosive energy. It did not escape my observation that he went around unarmed.

While we waited for the trading post to open, I briefed Red Fern on all the developments at the cabin and gave him his share of the gold I had panned and sluiced in Nugget Creek. Melville went back to stand guard under the treed cubs.

"What are your plans, Bob?" the Indian asked.

"Pretty uncertain. Thought I might paddle south somewhere—say the east bank—and build a cabin where I could winter with the cubs."

"How about the Takla Lake country—Northwest Arm? Cabin there where the river comes in. Belongs to a friend of mine here in Topley. There's gold in the stream bed. Hills are full of food for the cubs. Not so much effect of the drought. Richer country than Babine. You'll never see a soul, and you can't get out once winter sets in."

"What'll I do for supplies?"

"Take everything now for winter. I'll be up as soon as the ice melts. I'll bring enough for all summer. Outboard in by way of Stuart Lake."

"Sounds complicated."

"Not really. It'll be hell to get there. Specially the portage between Tahlo and Friday lakes. Steep ridge. Bad trail. Bad rapids between Friday and Nakinilerak lakes. Even worse for two miles down Hautête Creek below Natowite Lake. You could go in from the portage trail between Babine and Stuart, but you couldn't pole a canoe up the Stuart and Middle rivers. Takes two men or an outboard.

"You'll have to make your own furniture. Cabin hasn't been used in years. Needs repairs but beats having to build one from zero. And don't be a fool, Bob. Take my gun. Wolf packs, lions, grizzlies—even blacks—and wolverines will ambush you on the trail or tear that cabin down to get at you and the cubs and your food. You don't know what that Takla Lake country is like, 'specially in winter, 'cause wolves and lions and wolverines don't hibernate. And another thing, I don't trust Sarsis or Kaskas. Can't remember when a white prospector had ever come out of that country, alive or otherwise. Mounted Police don't even go in there. And they're even more locoed about bears than these Babines and Sekanis."

I looked back at the tree where three gray mudballs were crouching on a heavy branch and grimacing toward me with puzzled expressions. They had licked the mud from their little black snoots but were otherwise as dirty as before. Clete Melville was leaning against the tree, talking with a mill foreman.

"I'll head right for Takla Lake, Red Fern, but I won't take the gun. Thanks."

The order of five hundred pounds of food was boxed and about ready to be hauled to the jetty when another commotion began, this time on the front porch of the trading post. I opened the door and there were the cubs snapping and slinging their paws at a crowd of milling, chattering children and three baying dogs. When they saw me, the muddy bears rushed inside, grabbing apples, carrots, and a blackberry pie as they made a tumultuous, mud-shaking round of Hank's immaculate store. Attempting to stop Dusty as she retreated with a bunch of turnips in her mouth, I tripped over a bushel-basket of apples and sprawled out with a calamitous thud. The noise, the rolling apples, and my position on the floor frightened the cubs, who interpreted the fracas as an attempt to force them to surrender their loot. Dusty and Scratch followed Rusty up an avalanche of canned goods, boxed cereals, and catsup to an empty top shelf, where they proceeded to eat whatever they were carrying without once taking their eyes off me. Fortunately Hank Morgan had a sense of humor. Broken bottles of catsup, pickles, chili sauce, and mustard were all in the day's work as long as I was footing the bill. Most of my summer's gold was thus weighed out on Hank's scales.

"I'll help you get the bears to the landing," Red Fern offered. "Hank and Clete will bring your supplies in the truck. My hunch is that some of these hotheads are looking for trouble. You probably haven't heard this area'll probably be turned into a game refuge or a provincial park. The Indians are split right down the middle on the subject. Afraid the whites are going to take away more hunting and trapping rights."

Using a stepladder, I coaxed the cubs off the shelf, handed Scratch to Red Fern, put Rusty under one arm and Dusty under the other, and started back down the muddy thoroughfare to the dock. The apologetic Barney, from whom the cubs had escaped in the first place, was still sitting in the canoe.

"They all three piled overboard and swum ashore," he said. "I heard there was a little slammock."

"Well . . ." I said, after which I engaged each bear individually in a never-to-be-forgotten scrubbing. Somehow I suppressed the urge to spank.

A very handsome, erect Indian man in his early sixties walked up and introduced himself as Peter A-Tas-Ka-Nay. There was genuine warmth in his smile.

"I own the cabin you plan to use at the mouth of Hautête Creek." Apparently he and Red Fern had worked it all out before my arrival. "Red Fern and Clete say you are going to turn the bears loose when they're able to fend for themselves. Is that right?"

I was impressed by the softness of his voice and the unfathomable depth of his big brown eyes. Around his neck he wore a piece of polished mistletoe wood, northern talisman for old age and health. In the brilliant sunlight, his long, gray braids seemed to hang like a pair of snakes from beneath his broadbrimmed black felt hat.

"That's exactly the plan," I said, "to establish them on a range of their own where they can take care of themselves, in an area where there aren't any hunters. Will you please tell your people here that I am neither domesticating these bears nor training them for captivity?"

"I shall," he promised. "You are welcome to use my cabin as many years as you like. Most gold is at the outlet of Natowite Lake and the mouth of Hautête Creek. I'll help Red Fern bring in supplies in April. My son Larch has a cabin across the lake. He'll see you after the freeze when he comes in to tend his trap lines. Within this year we hope the Takla Lake region will be Takla Provincial Park. No hunting, no trapping."

"How far is your cabin, Mr. A-Tas-Ka-Nay?"

"Shortest way, one hundred ten miles. One four-mile

portage, otherwise downstream all the way. Don't try to paddle the lakes in high wind. Very hazardous for one man in a canoe. Better cordelle the rapids."

He sat down, removed a many-times-folded Department of Lands and Forests Pre-Emptor Series map from his hip pocket, traced my route with a pencil, and handed it to me. "Very easy to get lost in British Columbia bush. This here will show the way." He pointed to some gathering clouds above the hills east of Babine Lake. "Clouds are the tepees of all prospectors' dreams."

When the canoe was loaded and balanced with my regular gear plus the winter food supply, the bears, and me, it weighed three quarters of a ton, leaving a dangerous six-inch freeboard with which to face the wind-feathered surface of the lake. Village children, squaws, and some of the older men brought gifts of pemmican, jerky, corn pone, sow belly, and roe meal for the bears. The slanting afternoon light sketched deep character lines in their sun- and wind-whittled faces.

Hank Morgan and Clete Melville had convinced some of the Babines that my intentions were honorable as far as the bears' future was concerned, but huddles of disbelievers still muttered undertones in the street near the end of the jetty. Four dangerous-looking young men with rifles, including the teen-ager whose dog had been wounded in the fight, boarded a long bateau. After starting the motor, they headed for the center of the lake. They had declined to speak.

As I paddled back up the lake, each cub, one at a time, as if with goading conscience, scrambled over the mound of supplies to get astern in order to lick my face, make individual peace, and be reassured that I was not permanently angry at the fiasco they had precipitated in Topley Landing. As much as an adequate, natural diet of food, I reflected, these cubs needed games—physical and mental; approval—even of an avalanche inside the neatest store in the North Wood's; self respect, genuine affection, healthy competition, and an occasional muddy arena for letting off steam.

As usual, perceiving their care-free cubhood, I was chiefly concerned with maintaining those springs of unequivocal joy.

5

Faraway Pasture

For the long journey between Topley Landing on Ba-bine Lake and Peter A-Tas-Ka-Nay's cabin on Takla Lake, I budgeted twelve to fourteen days. Ordinarily 110 canoe miles could be accomplished on the lakes within three days, including siestas. The heavy load and the need for constant attention to the bears and robins, however, accounted for innumerable extra hours. The route was complicated, the portages time consuming, the cordelles backbreaking, and the head winds frustrating.

Following the western shoreline of Babine Lake for about twenty-five miles north of Topley Landing, I decided to cross where Green Arrow Peninsula jutted out to form a narrows. At that point the lake was but three miles wide and could be safely crossed in early morning before the wind swells began to roll. I planned to continue north along the eastern shoreline to the intake.

At the end of the northeast arm, a wildly dashing stream entered. I knew what kind of task I could expect in cordelling the heavy cargo—tugging the canoe behind me on a rope as I waded upstream a mile and a half to Morrison Lake. At the upper end of Morrison, I knew the job would have to be repeated along a greater white-water distance to Tahlo Lake.

Once across Tahlo—so I had been told—I could expect
to find an ancient Indian migration trail that paralleled
a spur of the Bait Range before zigzagging down a
precipitous ridge into the valley of Friday and
Nakinilerak lakes. . . . Although this portage was but
four miles in length, I knew from past experience that
it would take at least four sixteen-hour days—sixteen
round trips of eight miles each. In those days no one
considered the moving of four loads in an eighty-pound
pack too formidable for a 160-pound man in the
prime of youth and vigor. The canoe, an eighteen-
foot Peterborough, weighed seventy-nine pounds
empty. After the laborious portage, according to Red
Fern, there would be rapids and cataracts of unknown
character the length of Nakinilerak and Hautête
creeks.

Ten minutes north of Topley Landing we were once
again within the wilderness fastness of a world where
men still marked time by sunrise, high noon, sunset,
campfire, and unhurried sleep—a land replete with
room enough and time enough for timber wolves and
coyotes to sing their ancient songs—a big, sprawling,
healthy land of four distinct, power-packed seasons,
intimacy with which no true son of the north woods
could or would wish to escape. I watched the late
afternoon tailwind trickle through the cubs' coats as
they sat on hotly contested choice vantage points in
the canoe, staring in wonder at the number and variety
of living beings along the shoreline. In turn, every
animal ashore stared back at us. Red squirrels were
beginning early to pile their six-foot autumn stacks
of conifer cones, and picas were tedding their grass
harvest along the rims of rocky cliffs.

The four uncourtly Indians with rifles slowly
followed us for the rest of the afternoon, then quite
suddenly turned and gunned their outboard back
toward Topley Landing. Within an hour Clete Melville
and Red Fern arrived in Clete's motor launch to spend
an hour at our campfire.

I reviewed the several reasons for going to such a
remote and difficult region as Takla Lake. In addition

to the possibility of profitable gold panning, I was convinced it would be an ideal place to raise the cubs and free them as adult bears. To grow normally in their own habitat, they needed a natural bear diet which could be found only on a range of bogs, meadows, and forest, far from the competition now compressed into the unburned, drought-blighted areas near Babine Lake.

A wild bear grows to maturity and stays healthy for his twenty-five or thirty years on a vigorous program of physical exercise and diet unparalleled for any animal of his weight. I've watched both black and grizzly bears swim across the lake three miles wide, then climb over a mountain on the other side when easy alternative routes were available to them. I have seen black bears gallop down a mountainside and ascend a 200-foot fir without even breaking their speed—climbing by throwing their arms and legs around the trunk like a pole-climber—until they were near the top of the tree. The new region promised unlimited opportunity for the development of their ursine energy.

A further reason for accepting A-Tas-Ka-Nay's offer was the fact that the Takla Lake country offered thousands of square miles of high, almost impenetrable mountains, dense forest, and wild, unnavigable rivers where long-range precision rifles with telescopic sights ought to be generations away. Even if Parliament were reluctant to legislate the proposed national park, the creation of a game refuge in this section of British Columbia was virtually certain. Heavy pressure from conservation-minded organizations was being exerted on Ottawa. Farsighted Canadians refused to sit by and allow the same things to happen to their plant and animal life that had wiped out entire wild populations in the United States and created irreconcilable imbalances—and unpardonable injustices.

Crossing the Babine Lake narrows so as to reach the shoreline of Green Arrow Peninsula was not the easy feat I had pictured. On the second morning north of Topley Landing, I had paddled scarcely a mile over a glassy smooth surface when a snappy wind scud quartered the bow and threatened to capsize the canoe. Within moments the swells whipped up to three feet high and the spray forced the cubs to seek shelter under the seat. The rise of the bow over each crest and the slap of the bottom in the trough between waves terrified me as well as the cubs. An upset in the middle of the lake in that wind would be difficult to survive, not to mention losing one's equipment and means of locomotion.

The first wave to break over the bow and slosh five gallons of water into the cubs' faces sent them grumbling and climbing over duffle and grocery boxes in an all-out effort to get astern. Their long faces pointing straight ahead as solemn as Pilgrims', they settled down between my thighs. A rolling, pitching canoe with only one paddle for steering is one of the most unmanageable craft afloat. With knees planted wide apart against the bottom of the hull and leaning back against the seat, I maintained precious balance in spite of the squirming, stern-faced cubs. I had no choice but to face the wind and fight with every muscle in my body to keep the gale from spinning us into a broadside roll and the inevitable capsizing. We were beyond the point of no return.

Numb with cold and fright, I soon gave up the idea of forward locomotion. Even the battle to stay afloat, sculling the bow into the wind with the eight-inch blade, and bailing out between gusts, seemed mostly a losing one. Without all that cargo to act as ballast, the canoe would have overturned within five minutes. The slightest shift of gear would have effected the same result. At times I pulled against the cedar paddle loom until it bent. The twisting gale would not alow enough time to extricate one of the spares from the duffle in case of a broken padde.

After what seemed like a sizable chunk out of forever, the blasts diminished in duration and lost some of their punch. As I dug the blade into the lusty crests and cursed my aching shoulders, I finally became aware of some slight forward progress. The dark rim of the eastern shoreline slowly grew into individual conifers, rocks, precipices, and beach. When rational thought and hope returned, I dimly noted that my skin was drenched and blue with cold. I was shivering beyond any capability of further coordinated action.

Near the cliffs of the arrow-shaped jetty of land there was some protection; at least the danger of drowning was over. As luck would have it, no camp site was immediately available. Extremely old and lichened cedars and hemlocks stood in a forest now mature with spruce, balsam, and lodgepole pine. The rocky, narrow beach was overhung with alder and willow thickets. Dense riparian stands of balsam poplars (cottonwoods) six feet in diameter permitted only a few steep-angled spotlights of sunshine to search for the earth somewhere beneath the cavernlike gloom between crowded trunks. Wood ibises, herons, and bitterns stood like garrison sentries on skeletons of sun-blanched driftwood along the narrow fringe of beach, while from the treetops bald eagles and ospreys loudly decried our approach.

When at length we rounded a sharp headland and entered a long, fingerlike cove, I rejoiced at the sight of miles of peat bog and swampland where the cubs could root out a meal of insects, grubs, frogs, bulbs, tender basil shoots, skunk cabbage roots, and slimy yellow slugs. The nearest protected tent site was half a mile beyond the bay and difficult to approach in the wind due to the stony beach which could damage the heavy canoe. Late monkey flowers, columbines, asters, and paintbrushes simulated a deceptive atmosphere of spring.

While I set up camp and bear-proofed my provisions, the cubs were describing wider and wider arcs away from camp as they foraged over the new territory. I was about ready to join them for a hike into the bog when Rusty discharged a redoubtable whoop that could have been heard for a quarter mile. To guide me to him, he continued to bawl in cries that sounded like "Maw! Maw!" When I arrived, the trio was clinging to the topmost branch of a young spruce that swayed perilously under their weight. Heckling them with forearm passes was a large three-year-old black bruin who had climbed after the cubs as far as he dared without breaking the tree. The cubs saw me before the intruder did, and their soft gurgling caused him to turn his head to investigate the suddenly soft-pedaled cries of bloody murder. When the bear saw me, he immediately slipped down the trunk of the tree. I gave him enough room in which to escape without any feeling of being cornered or disgraced. To a bear, loss of face represents genuine calamity. Within his local society, withdrawal from any struggle most generally incurs loss of pecking rights—the established wilderness protocol of who has the right to clobber whom.

The three-year-old was not about to concede freeloading off his range without a battle. When Rusty, Dusty, and Scratch descended at my call, the bear roared back to evict my frightened friends, who cowered on their hind legs, hugging my knees and hissing. Reaching down for a four-foot length of squaw wood, I didn't retreat an inch as he heaved in for a fight. To report it honestly, I was wishing I had accepted Red Fern's offer of a gun. I didn't dare let the bear know how concerned I really was. An unflinching look squarely into his eyes, a slowly rising chunk of wood, and an Indian yell learned from my father turned the young boar toward the hill. As the stick overtook him and broke across his fat, round rump, he yelped as if he had been mortally wounded. I kept within sight as he circled back toward camp, where I hoped he would not seek a well-deserved revenge.

As we edged our way single file down into the boggy flat, I noticed how unstable the earth became. I attributed it to layers of peat as well as a deep carpet of sphagnum moss. Instead of lingering behind as was his habit before the forest fire, Scratch bounded and loped ahead as if enjoying the springy surface. Dusty, who was not far behind, only partly showed Scratch's high spirits. Rusty was still engaged in the more serious business of turning over sticks and stones for succulent grubs and crunchy beetles. Venturing onto a sandbar with many tracks of ducks and geese on it, Dusty and

Scratch became instantly mired. The last thing I would have expected was quicksand, yet there it was.

Unable to reach the struggling, steadily sinking cubs, I began to hurl sticks and large clumps of sphagnum moss for them to grab onto. The debris helped keep their heads and forearms above the jellylike surface of the stinking ooze, but neither bear was able to get within my reach. At length I worked a long, half-rotten branch across the pit of the sand, and both cubs got their arms around it. Rusty tried to crawl out on the branch in an apparent attempt to help, but I yanked him back by the tail. Dusty and Scratch seemed exhausted; they could not pull their bodies from the gulping mire. All at once I realized why they had become so debilitated. Big bubbles were rising to the surface of the quicksand, bursting, and slowly asphyxiating the cubs with swamp gas, a deadly poison more fatal than the quagmire itself. A young fir about six inches in diameter grew on one edge of the sand bar. Estimating that the cubs could live about ten minutes, and calculating the running time back to camp to get the ax and return, I decided to take the chance. When I returned, Rusty was sitting near the tree with his nose pointed skyward, whining as if his world had come to an end.

Once the tree was felled across the sump, I crawled out on the trunk, extracted both groggy, vomiting cubs, and placed them on the sphagnum carpet above the scene of their misadventure. After their recovery, we all walked down to the beach and took a much-needed bath.

Those bears were always demonstrative of their appreciation—a sort of built-in refinement. They exaggerated the trait with hugs, gurgles, and licks each time they were delivered from imbroglios which they recognized as critical. After such rescues, I could generally count on a breather of exemplary behavior for about twenty-four hours.

The Green Arrow Peninsula of Babine Lake was twelve miles long. Across from the capehead, nestled in the crotch of the Y of the northwest and northeast arms of the lake, was the all but abandoned Indian hamlet of Old Fort. The hangers-on were winter trappers and summer fishermen, miserably housed, poorly clothed, ill-fed but happy, handsome, intelligent people. Their lives were uncomplicated by twentieth-century gadgets and stomach ulcers. Half a dozen children, three squaws, and four toothless old men came down to the beach to greet me but ran toward the woods when the cubs raised their growling little heads and cocked ears above the gunnels. I was able to coax the men back for a pleasant visit, but the women and children hid behind trees where they revealed only half a head and one eye.

It was good to be on the northeast arm because the lake was narrower, the scenery more luxuriantly mountainous, and the beaches of decomposed granite more approachable for soft, broadside landings and launchings. Night and day the late summer air was heavy with the fragrance of balsam, whose sugary syrup exuded and dripped from the maturing pine cones at this time of year. The bogs and creek banks were brilliant with giant lemon lilies that extravagantly expended a fortune in perfume not unlike that of a California lemon orchard. The early morning air had a sharp bite to it that made it delicious to breathe.

From mountainous escarpments above every weathered bend along our course, pure white mountain goats—zoologically antelopes—and golden Dall sheep shook their heavy heads as the canoe parted a slow V-wake across the dark-purple depths. Moose slopped around and harvested the soft roots of plantain and water lily from the tangles of reedy inlets. Deer, wapiti, and caribou does and fawns grazed on alder and willow shoots near the shore, while their bucks looked down from the high, barren shoulder ridges grown with "shintangle" yew. Now and then a bear reared to swap distant argument with the cubs. Sometimes throwing me off balance, chinook salmon swimming aft of the stern would seize the shiny copper paddle-shoe.

Bird songs, proclaiming squatters' rights. surged from every willow brake and sphagnum muskeg. Distant sentinel bucks and bulls bugled to alert their harems to our passing.

The north woods themselves were a living symbol of inviolable space, ageless solitude, and comfortable permanence. The trumpetings of bull moose and the barely audible calls of a pair of rock wrens—who always sang together or not at all—blended in perfect harmony with what appeared to be an entire continent of vast, rolling forest. The robins in the carton beneath the canoe seat reminded me of feeding time every two hours, and the three cubs' little black faces with black leather snoots stared back from the bow with measurably growing affection and quick response to their names when I called them. Despite the rudeness with which nature had evicted us from our pleasant Nugget Creek home, and the uncertainties facing us in the Takla region, I felt a genuine warmth at being even momentarily important to these seven little creatures of the Canadian bush.

On the lake I had plenty of time to think about Clete Melville, Red Fern, and A-Tas-Ka-Nay. How very different they were, yet a pattern of calm and strength characterized all three. Nothing could cause any one of them to shout, rush madly about, or lose his temper. They were rough men of the north who had assailed and survived the north's unconstrained violence; on the other hand, they had delivered babies with the gentleness of a nun. One scarcely noticeable incident, which had gone almost unobserved at the time, crossed and recrossed my recollection. When Clete Melville and Red Fern visited my camp that first night out of Topley Landing, Clete had jumped from his launch and with one powerful hand had lifted the bow and pulled the heavy craft ashore. With the same hand, he had picked up a wood ant and handed it to a curious horned lark that had run across the sand to investigate his arrival.

The noisy creek, too shallow and swift to paddle, flowed into the northernmost bay of Babine Lake. The right bank of the stream being somewhat less rocky, I cordelled the boat up that side by a bow rope fixed to a ring through a metal hondo. During that cordelling, the bears were in and out of the boat so often they became one hell of a nuisance; each wet cub, boarding and reboarding, could skillfully spread a half gallon of water and mud over three quarters of the contents of the boat each time it got in and out. For the entire journey, however, they never jumped from the canoe as long as I was paddling open water from the stern seat.

Morrison Lake, almost unapproachable by boat, lay in a slender fourteen-mile-long basin at the bottom of a deep, winding canyon. I was sorely tempted to remain on the shore of that remote and beautiful lake because of its primitive setting in the southern Bait Range of the Omineca Mountains. In addition to the lake's natural charm, an impressive parade of animal life foraged up and down its shoreline. Some of that number may have swum Babine during the forest fire. Their expressions and bearings no longer showed any of the unmistakable marks of terror and urgency.

The moving presence of all this four-legged life frequently upset the cubs. One playful otter in an aspen dam near one of our camps persisted in heckling a colony of beavers simply because the latter manifested so little interest in self-defense. Over and over again the bears pursued the otter from one end of the pool to the other, attempting to catch what they considered a pest. At the end of the chase—outswum, outrun, outmaneuvered—the trio staggered back into camp defeated, worn to the quick, and crankier than pinched hornets. It was their first taste of total defeat, a frustrating embarrassment not to be lived with graciously.

The night I camped where the combined drainage streams of Haul and Tahlo lakes enter the upper neck of Morrison Lake, I remembered one of Red Fern's admonitions: "It is dangerous to travel in the bush only if you are in the company of young animals." As an Indian he knew that bear cubs were fair game for grizzlies, cougars, wolves, wolverines, eagles, lynx, even coyotes and martens. If hunting in pairs or more, the larger predators might attack a man with bear cubs should hunger or the memory of a previous taste of juicy, young bear flesh become acute. My reason for recalling Red Fern's warning was an encircling pack of seven timber wolves. I kept the cubs up a fir that evening and built my campfire about six feet from the bole of the tree. I suspected they would slide down to crawl into the sleeping bag with me as soon as I hit the sack. I even considered spending the night in the tree with them, and would have done so had another idea not occurred to me. I decided to use Rusty to bait the wolves into camp for the well-known Canadian double-cross. When the cub was in my lap near the glowing embers of the fire, Dusty and Scratch began to bleat and whine for permission to descend. Their cries were part of my sinister plan to whet lupine appetites. By moonlight I observed the cautious approach of four monstrous scouts.

"Tree!" I whispered to Rusty, placing him against the trunk. As he obeyed and shinnied up the bark, the wolves rushed in and tried to grab him before he could get out of reach. With a short-handled shovel I delivered four loads of hot coals into their thick fur before they could retreat. Howls of pain and surprise broke up the stalemate. I heard them yelp as they plunged again and again into the lake to extinguish their torment. The pack moved down the valley for less hazardous hunting.

The bears and I were awakened just before sunrise when the robins began to shriek in their carton, which I had placed between the sleeping bag and the well-stoked fire. I never knew what might creep, fly, or crawl into camp; but whoever the visitor might be, or however silent his approach, those little birds never failed to sound the alert. During daylight and early evening, the cubs were more vigilant than a hound; but when we went to bed they surrendered that duty and turned all responsibility for safety over to me. I in turn entrusted the robins with the job of sentinels. When the three cubs and I peeped out from the opening in the top of the sleeping bag that morning, we were horrified to see a weasel gnawing his way into the carton of screaming nestlings. One minute later would have been good-bye to the little birds.

"Get 'im!" was a signal the cubs had learned chasing lemmings on the meadows above Nugget Creek. As if shot from the mouth of a cannon, they left the sleeping bag as a unit and chased the predator away.

I had no difficulty finding the ancient Indian migration trail at the northern end of Tahlo Lake. The tour de force was in carrying almost three quarters of a ton over the four-mile ridge between Tahlo and Friday lakes. My packrack-rucksack combination was a modification of the light Trapper Nelson rig, famous during the days of the voyageurs when long portages were the order rather than the exception. Since I could not possibly walk the 128 miles of the sixteen necessary trips in less than four days, and since sixty-four miles of the journey would be covered under an average load of eighty pounds, I decided to attempt two trips on the afternoon of our arrival at the upper end of Tahlo Lake. Much of the little-used trail had to be cleared of deadfalls, fern, cat's-claw, and other growth; washouts and washins also demanded attention. Consequently, on the first trip with all the tools, it took me five hours just to reach the shore of Friday Lake, but the work I did on the trail made the other trips smoother. When we completed the second trip at midnight, the cubs were cranky and showed every cranky sign of fatigue. They had foraged the full sixteen miles; still, without the usual smoked salmon snack, they snapped and snarled as they settled down for the night.

I don't know why it worked out that way, but in the sleeping bag Rusty always stretched out the length of my back, monopolizing that side of the bag. Scratch cuddled up next to my stomach and chest until he got too warm. Then he would trade places with Dusty, especially if I turned over during the night. Whereupon Rusty would invariably reach up and give me a light lick across my nose, as if apologizing for being about to turn over so I could warm his back and in order that he might use my arm for a pillow.

All three cubs vied for individual attention. They loved a short romp in bed before going to sleep or getting up, above all if they had in mind to work me into a chest-and-belly-rubbing mood. They learned to stand in line, almost ritually, for an evening once-over in search of parasites: ticks, wood lice, fleas, leeches. They loved the touch of the human hand, which they associated with food, safety, and affection—sometimes information. We rarely sat around a campfire as four separate beings, but rather occupied a log or leaned against a boulder, often entwined as if we feared some common enemy.

Since early childhood, I've been a sucker for the pleas of wild animals, who have beaten a steady path to my tent flap and sleeping bag. My bedfellows have had four legs, two legs, and no legs; feathers, fur, or scales. There is no better way to know and develop rapport with any animal than to sleep with him!

During the four and a half days of the tiresome portage, I must in all honesty admit that at least once every hour I found myself questioning my own judgment and the possible results of the move to the distant lake. Items like sugar, flour, coffee, salt—packaged goods—had to be tarped against the weather, then hung from branches at Friday Lake to secure them against the ravages of animals. In spite of these precautions, I soon found that rats, squirrels, and wood ants were managing to climb up and down the ropes and raid the bundles and cartons. On one trip I arrived in the nick of time to frighten off a bull moose that was flipping the lowest of the suspended supplies back and forth with his antlers. Stacked cartons of canned foods, with some inevitable smell of food on them from other supplies, were fair game to be ripped open and scattered over the landscape by bears, wolverines, and coyotes.

Nevertheless the unbounded beauty of each day in the singing, timeless forest, as well as the endless antics of the cubs as they half-played, half-foraged along both sides of the trail, compensated in no mean measure for the endless miles of portaging, with its sweat, aches, doubts, and occasional forebodings.

Before attempting the white water between Friday and Nakinilerak lakes, I cut a long sapling fir three inches in diameter to be used as a drag pole as it dragged along the bottom, I had a very effective braking system. This old Indian technique worked fine down the first creek. The icy water of Hautête Creek below Nakinilerak Lake was abnormally low due to lack of snow and rain in the watershed. Exposed rocks were spaced in such an infernal pattern as to make canoeing all but impossible. There was no beach along either bank for lining or cordelling by rope. I was inching along through the noisy, frothy stream, the drag pole bouncing from stone to stone down the narrow channel, when the soft, young fir snapped about halfway down its nine-foot length. Leaning backward as I was, I fell heels over appetite into the roiling crests while the canoe continued down the shallow stream. Ramming the first obstruction—a sandbar—the craft swung broadside into a trough between waves, listed into the onrushing water, filled and foundered. As it did so I saw the cubs abandon ship and make for dry land, but I feared my helpless robins must surely have drowned. Reaching the swamped canoe, I fished the dripping carton from beneath the seat. The sweetest music I ever heard came from four coughing, squawking throats inside the water-logged box, which was now starting to disintegrate.

Item by item, I unloaded the canoe and deposited her cargo on a narrow strip of beach. Such essentials as sugar, flour, salt, cereals, and other spoilables were in waterproof, oiled-silk sacks, but the paper labels were beginning to float away from the canned goods, which meant surprise menus throughout the winter ahead. The sleeping bag was wrapped in a rubberized ground cloth, so it remained powder dry. On the other hand, all my winter clothing, packed in a canvas dufflebag, was soaked and too heavy to remove as a unit. When the last piece of gear and the canoe were ashore in the small embayment among cabin-size boulders, it was too late to plan to cover any more miles that day.

Blue and numb with cold and fatigue, I kept repeating the old cliché: "Courage alone is not enough up here." I was sitting next to a rock, shaking from head to foot, when I missed the cubs. The wet, shivering robins were clinging to the edge of their recently collapsed home, shrieking what I misinterpreted as a mere complaint about their housing problem. Cramming the unwilling birds back into their soggy quarters and covering them with a canvas tarp, I was about to get to my feet and take out after the bears, when I suddenly looked up a long dark leg about as tall as a totem pole. There were three more legs, equally impressive, that went with the first, and half a ton of black belly in between. The behemoth just stood there towering above me as I sat, and I still remember how he kept moving one ear back and forth as if he were undecided as to what to do. Seventy-five feet above his antlers, and on three separate branches, I spotted the curious but circumspect smiles of Rusty, Dusty, and Scratch.

Too bushed to move and almost beyond responsible thought and activity, I just leaned back against the boulder near the robins and waited for the moose to make up his mind. I was in no mood for a skirmish, mental or otherwise, with this feudal lord of the north. His unobserved approach, like the broken drag pole, demonstrated the acute suddenness with which the unforseeable can occur in the north woods. With the calm of a yoga, the moose proceeded to eat my winter supply of potatoes, then splashed away up the creek without ever having shown by any overt act that he recognized my existence. My reaction at the time was: "He could have given me at least one kick of satisfaction!"

Only after the scattered wreckage had been returned to a semblance of order and the soaked gear spread for drying did I consider preparing a meal for the birds and bears. I spent campfire time that night sewing up the seams of the robins' carton, which had come unglued during the dunking. It was wonderfully reassuring how the cubs had learned to respect off-limits orders where the robins were concerned, and equally remarkable that they had treed without orders when danger moved in.

The lower ten miles of Hautête Creek ran swift, narrow and deep—a canoeman's dream. Within the space of three hours I paddled the length of the L-shaped Natowite Lake and at the outlet reentered Hautête Creek, which poured along with twice the volume of its upper reaches, owing to contributions from the Taltapin Lake drainage basin to the south. Roughly ten miles below Natowite Lake, the riverlike Hautête Creek entered a wide bay of the Northwest Arm of Takla Lake. On a rise on the right bank some twenty yards above the stream, recessed an equal distance from the crystal-clear beach of the lake, stood the shake roof of a cabin. It looked like a ripe seed pod growing on top of the dense tangle known as forest understory.

6

Motley Associates

The cabin, with its makeshift kitchen, though spacious, was a disappointment in almost every way after I had spent two seasons in the comparative luxury of Red Fern's dwelling. Shrubbery, vines, and weeds had taken over the outside during the many years since the structure had been occupied by the Indians. Rats, mice, bats, snakes, a horde of assorted beetles had assumed tenancy inside; there was neither furniture nor facilities. In the ramshackle cupboard buzzed a hive of bees. You might say there was running water—when it rained through the roof. The floor was warped and piled high with pack-rat accumulations; the beamed ceiling—the underside of the roof—was hung with bull bats scowling from their upside-down perch. A family of ogling arctic owls swayed and hissed from a nest at one junction of corner joists and roof rafters. The door sagged ajar on corroded hinges. Still, there were no broken windowpanes, and the fireplace, aside from being clogged by a decade of cobwebs, fallen leaves, and other debris, appeared operational.

Within the first ten minutes the cubs had devoured the bee hive—honey, bees, and comb—and had scooped up every crawling, creeping creature except the snakes, which they chased out along with the owls and bats. They systematically tore up the pack rats' nests and crunched down the hapless occupants. It was during this wild fracas that I realized their remarkable growth and increasing strength.

The front room was about twelve by twenty feet with the cobblestone fireplace along the south wall. There was a small window on each side of the fireplace. Two large French windows in the north wall afforded ample light and a magnificent view of Takla Lake. The kitchen, like that in the Nugget Creek cabin, was a shed-type lean-to built onto the west end of the building. One sliding-pane window that offered a tiptoe view of the forest behind the dwelling completed the efficient lighting and ventilating system. Though of course it lacked running water, the kitchen had a sink and a rusty cast-iron stove. Someone in the past had tired of hauling buckets of water from the creek and had piped the commodity from a distant pool for a continuous gravity-flow supply at the door. Strangely enough, a small trickle still dripped from the pipe.

Basically the building was solidly constructed and ideally situated. Immediately after unloading the canoe, I began the overwhelming job of clearing and repairing it. Fortunately there were tools, nails, extra shingles, and finish lumber in a tool and firewood shed at the rear of the cabin. The one place safe from all forms of animal life was the hide cache in the back yard, a small, weatherproof cubicle on a platform at the top of four, well-anchored logs twelve feet tall. The last three feet of each post was wrapped with galvanized sheet metal, making entry impossible for any animal. The thiefproof vault on the platform had been built years before to house the harvest of A-Tas-Ka-Nay's trap lines as well as to store his winter supply of food. The door could be reached only by ladder. When my own supplies were cached there, I decided it would be a safe temporary harbor for the robins. To develop the habit of removing the ladder each time I used the cache, I printed a sign on a shingle and hung it between the fifth and sixth rungs where I could not help reading it as I stepped to the ground: "Remove me!" Northern predators were masters in the art of ladder climbing.

With all the squatter tenants evicted or devoured, I devoted most of the daylight hours to repairs, building furniture, clearing the yard of wild growth; sawing, splitting, and stacking the winter fuel supply; fishing, and smoking trout, kokanee, and squawfish. I spent each morning establishing a reliable forage range for the cubs. I even found time to extent the front overhang of the cabin and to replank the porch where we could sit of an early evening and watch the changing lights on the Y of the two arms of dazzling blue Takla Lake. The late afternoon sunlight burnishing the endless spread of the Omineca peaks to the east along the Continental Divide was a source of daily joy and relaxation.

The robins—technically red-breasted thrushes—had now become what I am tempted to call real personalities, individuals whose moods were always legible in the attitudes of their tattered little tail feathers. After their moult of chick plumage, a crop of pinfeathers suddenly burst forth into full summer dress. As fledglings they were impatient with their dark prison tower. Almost overnight my task of weaning them from their dependency upon me became urgent. They had to learn fear and how to evade a forestful of natural enemies. I built them a wooden box with a platform shelf against the sunny afternoon side of the cabin where they could retreat out of reach of predators. They were quick to learn that a hop and a flap easily achieved safety from the three nosey little bears whom I trusted with everything but robins. For a week the birds roosted at night on the mantel above the fireplace, but they soon came to prefer the shelf out of doors.

Treeing the cubs, I placed the birds in a circle around pinebark scales. They soon began to watch the twig with which I turned over the scale to reveal to them the hiding places of juicy sawyers, miller larvae, and slug eggs. After several such demonstrations, they were turning over their own forest chips and fighting over the spoils. When I set them on deadfalls and pulled away bits of sphagnum, they pounced upon fleeing ants and earwigs. Before I realized that Nature's strongest force, instinct, was at work as my infallible ally, the robins rushed to remove the moss from every deadfall upon which I set them. Teaching them to dig for worms and slugs along the moist collar of the creek took much longer. They could see the twig turn the bark scale; they could get the idea of pulling sphagnum with their beaks. But actually digging with both feet tried their patience and mine before it could be put into practice. I had to wait until they were exhausted from hunger, show them a succulent worm, and bury it in front of their eyes before they engaged beaks and claws in the physical act of unearthing it. While they watched, I removed the droppings of mammals in the game trails to reveal to them that manure harbors a variety of bugs. They followed me to patches of ripening raspberries, blueberries, and red pods of eglantine that festooned over both banks of the creek. They shrieked and flapped their wings as if instinctively bluffing away such competition as cedar waxwings and tanagers. After learning to dig, it wasn't long before they were experimenting with clumps of millet, wheat grass, rye, timothy, and clover, where tasty seeds could be thrashed out with wings and claws.

One afternoon I was sawing a fallen spruce into sections for splitting. The four robins sat sunning themselves on another log I had rolled down the hill south of the cabin. The cubs were asleep on the shady side of the dwelling. The first hint of danger came too late. A duck hawk, sighting the plump birds on the log, swooped silently down, taloned one of my friends, and just as swiftly flew to the top of a nearby pine with the screaming victim. Her dying cries for help remained in my ears for days, like the songs of the larks who had perished in the fire along with the robins' parents and the hermit thrushes.

When I rushed to the log, waving my arms and shouting to frighten the three remaining robins into the underbrush, they flew to my shoulders and chirped in my ears as was their custom.

Predators killed and ate robins every day. I had steeled my daily feelings against that incomprehensible side of nature that equipped certain animals to slaughter others and live off their flesh. When the cubs killed and ate animals I accepted it as somehow tied in with population control. When *my* robin was killed, the act became murder.

Although the cubs at that time weighed approximately fifty pounds each, I knew they were still being considered by two bald eagles who inhabited a giant alder on the left bank of Hautête Creek. In addition to trout and salmon, the big birds with the eight-foot wingspread regularly brought in hares, marmots, squirrels, and snakes. They circled and banked very near the cubs each time we walked down the beach, until finally one day I hit the male eagle with a rock. After that they decided to hunt a less risky diet.

Grown bears in the Takla Lake region foraged between six and eight hours a day, depending upon the provender of their ranges, the proximity to hibernation, and the competition—real or imagined. On a diversified, five- to seven-mile range, including riparian, bog, meadow, savannah, and silvan acreage, I discovered that the triplets could generally satiate themselves within three hours. When they began to cavort on their hind legs and toss a field mouse back and forth between them instead of gulping it almost without chewing, I knew the little round bellies would last for at least another twenty-four hours. Table scraps being a nonexistent integer in my frugal prospector's fare, the bears had soon learned that begging during my own meals would produce no results. Therefore, except for one smoked fish per evening, they were no longer dependent upon domestic food by the time September arrived.

We generally began our early morning foraging with a walk along the clean, sandy beach of Takla Lake. About half a mile south of the cabin, a freshet seeped into the lake from a ten-acre bog of grasses, sedges, cattails, reeds, spike rushes, and a wild berry vine I was never able to identify. The bog had also felt the pinch of drought and chinook wind, but seepages on the Takla watershed continued to trickle and the creeks, although low, showed no sign of drying up. One day after frightening a yearling bear out of the bog, the cubs excitedly began prying into his affairs. They discovered that he had been digging the rhizomes of camas and a plant not unlike eastern arrowroot. Ever afterward they sought and dug the goodies wherever they could find them.

As they bounded and clawed their way through the bog, I couldn't help comparing their voluminous activity with that of the self-satisfied bitterns who stood motionless for hours on end and followed other creatures' activities almost without moving their eyes. When the presumptuous cubs approached too closely, hoping to flush the birds into flight, the bitterns made forceful speeches which sent the cubs hightailing back to me, whining for me to intercede.

Beyond the bog we followed a level game trail through dense forest where the sphagnum-carpeted litter was surprisingly alive with the crunchiest of bugs and juiciest of larvae. The forest thinned out toward the crest of the hill where stands of spruce exposed from the south opened into a mile-wide meadow with an ice-cold spring near the center. We never loitered long on that meadow, because it was too far from a tall tree in case the owner of the grizzly bear tracks should decide upon fresh cub for breakfast. I had heard unverified Indian reports that this sometimes happened.

Contrary to popular notion, I knew that a grizzly could climb a tree the same as a black bear, but that he wouldn't trust his eight hundred pounds on a slender branch. From the amount of feathers strewn about, it was plain that the elderly grizzly was attracted by the numerous stupid but tasty spruce hens. These fowl, a species of grouse, would allow most animals to approach them; it looked as if the birds were imploring extermination. I was inwardly delighted the day one ruffled cock turned and pecked Rusty on the nose, then chased Dusty and Scratch out of the meadow in a wild melee of cackles, whoops, and bellows. I herded the cubs away when I remembered that the disturbance might interrupt the grizzly's siesta.

En route back to the cabin, we habitually explored the deep spear grass and late-ripening cranberries in a mile of cottonwood savannah before taking what I called the sundown game trail along the right bank of Hautête Creek. Deer, bighorn sheep, elk, woodland caribou, and wolves used to follow that trail to the lake each day just before twilight.

Too often Scratch had to be called out of his day-dreaming way of lingering behind, while Rusty occasionally required admonition for getting too far ahead. Dusty was still the ideal walking companion in that she almost never strayed twenty feet from my heels. On the hikes Rusty was fiercely independent, seriously businesslike, and thoroughly dependable. From the beginning, he assumed his own variety of responsibility in looking out for the rest of us; and Scratch, especially, enjoyed every moment of being looked out for. To Dusty, self-reliance apparently seemed a state to be avoided at all costs, even though I spent more and more time and energy on that specific phase of the cubs' education. The last mile of each day's walk was most rewarding for me: the cubs were full, anxious to get home, and very easy to march single file down the trail. Nevertheless, they often bumped into one another, no doubt secretly hoping to provoke fisticuffs.

The old fly-up-the-creek heron, who lived on a right-bank jetty of rock and reeds half a mile above the cabin, generally crossed to the left bank just prior to our arrival and passing. On several occasions the big wader slapped Rusty's face with his wing, but he always flapped away when I got within fifty feet. I admired the beauty of his slow, effortless flight, but equally disliked the flat croak of his call, which no doubt was sweet music to his heroness.

Our motley wild associates included a small flock of haughty Canada geese who for some reason preferred the sandy right bank of Hautête Creek where the stream poured into the lake. It struck me that the innate dignity of a Canada goose was indestructible. If bears were the democrats of north woods society, geese were the true aristocrats through organization, discretion, and group pride. The cubs had more intuition than to approach the sandbar dominion of the geese.

The embodiment of vanity, the hens preened their feathers and gossiped while the ganders paraded back and forth like cavaliers in front of their ladies long beyond the mating and nesting season. Whenever a lark or song sparrow would broadcast an aria from the cabin roof or a nearby spruce, the geese would waddle over to the water for a short regatta as if to remind the tree-dwellers, "Maybe we can't carry a tune, but *you* can't swim." During each display of adult snobbery, the goslings led me to suspect them of playing a naughty little game of "mix-up," because when the mothers returned to the sandbar, there was vicious pecking and feather pulling until the intimate little community untangled the filial dilemma and determined which butterball belonged to whom.

Early one morning a lynx crept onto the rearing grounds and seized the mother of one of the largest families. The decoys had been unable to lure the predator toward themselves. An unwed hen immediately adopted the orphans and cared for them until migration.

The decoy system further attests the fierce devotion conspicuous within this laudable aristocracy. Canada geese wed for life. If either mate is killed, the survivor assumes the role of flock decoy, whose irrevocable

duty it becomes thereafter to attract and seduce the
attention of the hunter—man or beast. The decoys
beguile intruders by feigning a broken wing or by
acting the part of the slow, the weak, the stupid.
Frequently I have observed these "suicide squads"
taking deliberate direction toward predators during
the flocks' critical moments before getting their fat
bodies airborne. A decoy always drops out of a flying
wedge to test the safety of an area before the flight
commander will allow the other birds to descend. The
mortality rate among the decoys is predictably high.

Several species of seed-eating associates—grouse,
pheasants, grosbeaks, and finches—resided near the
cabin. Local insectivores included larks, swallows,
phoebes, orioles, and a host of woodpeckers and wrens.
Flesh-eating birds besides hawks, eagles, owls, and
kingfishers were rare. I cannot recall ever having seen
a buzzard in northern British Columbia. Birds that
would eat almost anything—omnivores—were magpies,
whisky-jacks, ravens, robins, jays, and flocks of little
unidentifiables.

Never very far behind the flocks, herds, or individual
ungulates—regardless of season—were the big game
killers—wolves, coyotes, cougars. On the tail of every
rodent—hare, beaver, marmot, squirrel, or rabbit—were
fox, lynx, marten, wolverine, badger, mink, weasel,
and birds of prey. Some neighbors were known for
their extreme individuality—family-associated cleanup
committees—raccoons, skunks, otters, black and grizzly
bears. When the spawning season for chinook and
sockeye came in August, most carnivores went on a
fish diet.

One of the most attractive summer features of the
lake country was the general absence of mechanical
sounds. At night geese called, moose bugled, wolves
sang, sheep bleated, crickets fiddled, frogs croaked,
and owls hooted or screeched. From earliest light of
dawn on the dewy moors, when the curlews crowed,
until the brilliant and lingering northern twilight when
the marmots whistled back and forth from the shelf-
lands, there was no clear day in any season when the

air did not carry a measure of exuberance and melody.

Each animal species required a distinctly different type of range—often wide, varied, and hotly contested by both individuals of the same species and other genera as well. While the cubs served their apprenticeship in learning to find their own meals, they provided a vivid demonstration for me in the extent of all animal's range needs. Bullock's oriole, for example with an almost exclusive diet of certain caterpillars, worked a range of fifty square miles per day in order to meet his family needs. That's why we never saw an oriole perch very long in one place. He couldn't afford to squander time if he was to enjoy such a select, gourmet dinner. On the other hand, marmot, hare, and pica found sufficient forage for months within a few feet of their front doors.

For special treats, I slid the canoe into Hautête Creek and paddled across to a big hilly forest which belonged to another family of bears by virtue of earlier preemption. Biologically, it was known as a mature forest, because the entire region would support little more than was already growing or making a living there. On these occasions I never had to call Rusty, Dusty, and Scratch. They were aboard, gurgling their approval through outturned lips long before the canoe was ever launched. We recognized the ominous fact that these forays into somebody else's territory were loaded with risk of every known element of mayhem from the permanent residents. One morning, quite by chance, however, I discovered that during every poaching visit of ours to the neighbors' preserve, a mother bear and her two cubs crossed the creek above our route and pillaged our own established range for all they were worth. As luck would have it, the arrangement proved convenient all around: no one was ever confronted with any face-losing showdown. The five cubs and one adult bear were thus apparently afforded the opportunity to gorge that particular part of ursine appetite which must now and then be satisfied—a sort of inevitable compulsion toward larceny!

These raids on the left bank of the creek led us to

longer expeditions up the sixteen miles of the Northwest Arm of Takla Lake. Cliffs of solid limestone and beachless escarpments prevented as many landings as I would have liked, but the cubs enjoyed nothing more than leisurely gliding over the flat surface near the lake shore. They dug exotic larvae and roots and turned over stones in the creeks for hellgrammites they would have ignored at home, while I spaded up the "roots o' rainbows," as the oldtime prospectors put it, for a look at what gold flakes might have settled into crevices of bedrock.

One day at the upper narrows of the lake, I crossed to the eastern shore and paddled down the peninsula to the Y. A choppy wind got up and I was unable to attempt the five-mile crossing back to Hautête Creek until after sundown. The delay gave the bears the opportunity to climb the yellowing cliffs to the tall fir forest that grew above the two arms of the lake. At one rocky overview, I sat down for lengthy study of both arms, the Y, and the lower lake. Always on the lookout for signs of gold, platinum, berylium, and other minerals, I spent the next three days exploring every creek mouth along the fourteen miles to the outlet which was called Middle River.

Directly opposite the mouth of Hautête Creek, on the far shore of the Northeast Arm, we came upon a well-built spruce-log cabin which stood on a rise some forty yards back from the beach. Treeing the cubs after beaching, I walked up and entered the unlocked front door. The cabin had been occupied within the year. The cupboards were well-stocked with a winter's supply of canned food, and a lean-to shed just outside the kitchen housed the neatly stacked fuel wood. My stomach turned when I spotted three dozen assorted steel traps and chains hung in neat rows along the wall of the wood shed.

I saw no gain in taking the implements of torture to the middle of the lake and dumping them; the trapper would only order a new supply.

I have never heard the trapping business appropriately condemned.

Tearing a sheet of paper from my notebook and

scribbling a note on the rough-hewn table in the living room, I invited the trapper over to meet the cubs. From the construction of his snowshoes, homespun blankets on a moose-thong bed, articles from his winter whittling, and woven chinking between the logs of his walls, I knew he was an unmarried Indian. From an envious inspection of a shelf of books, I surmised that he was an educated young reader of philosophy, adventure, and natural history. I could not expect the appearance of a man of his trade before the snows of late November.

Babine Lake drains north by way of the Babine River, which flows into the Skeena, a mighty stream that empties into a fjord almost one hundred miles inland from Prince Rupert. Takla Lake, on the other hand, less than twenty air miles from Babine, drains by way of the Middle River, Trembleur and Stuart lakes into the Fraser River, which enters the Strait of Georgia and the Pacific Ocean at Vancouver. Indian traplines formed a network between the two drainage basins.

Summer greenery gradually blended into the artist's palette of September. All due precautions for an early winter had been taken: wood was cut and stacked alongside the cabin, snowshoes were greased, spaghnum chinking was tamped and plastered with mud inside and out, shutters were repaired, and food was packed into a sphagnum-insulated cellar under the kitchen to prevent freezing. Every day I invented excuses to spend more hours with the cubs. For one thing, the robins, like the shore birds, had migrated early, and their box on the shelf at the back of the cabin was a constant reminder that I missed them. I wondered how they would find their way for the first time down the long flyways to Sonora and Sinaloa. Perhaps it was because I felt their absence so keenly that I sought more time with the bears.

The cubs were conscious of two rather separate worlds: indoors and out. Somewhat stoically, they accepted my silly dicta against roughhousing, bad manners, temper tantrums, and displays of jealousy while indoors. These regulations were my defense against the day when a compound bear fight in the parlor might transform the entire cabin into irreclaimable debris. I recall one near calamity the afternoon Dusty slapped Scratch into a crock of sourdough "starter" that I kept on a low stool near the kitchen stove. It had been a miserably cold and drizzly day. The cubs had refused to go farther than a mile and had eaten practically nothing. Rusty and Dusty wanted to curl up by the hearth and sleep, but Scratch took it into his head to play. To avoid trouble, I coaxed him for a short walk down the beach. He danced, rolled in the sand, and tossed pieces of bark into the lake. Within ten minutes, however, he made a beeline back to the cabin. Even before I could wipe him dry with a large towel that I kept near the door for that purpose, he barged inside and grabbed Dusty by the heel. Without considering my rule against roughhousing indoors, she stood up and landed a haymaker alongside Scratch's head that sent him sprawling against the crock of sourdough, which whitewashed him from head to foot.

All three bears cringed, expecting physical reprisals in addition to my virulent verbal outburst. After a forceful dunking in the icy lake, Scratch spent the rest of the day as an outcast in the darkest corner under the bed.

Rusty's favorite indoor toy was the old blanket under which the robins used to sleep when they were half-naked fledglings. He would lie on his back in front of the fireplace and fold and unfold the frazzled old bed piece until I thought he would shred it; then he would chew it and roll on it or hide it under the bed, promising a swat for the slightest interest by Dusty or Scratch. They had learned how to distinguish between his serious and playful moods. From our first night in the A-Tas-Ka-Nay cabin, Rusty took his toy to bed with him. Dusty had found a driftwood maple burl on Babine Lake. It must have been sweet, for she gnawed and licked the bone-hard knot during every session of play with it. The toy was her indoor companion. Always remembering where she left it, she would curl up near Rusty with the kickshaw between her front paws. Sometimes she slept with it next to her chest. Scratch was low man of the totem pole of peck rights. He had no regular indoor toy and disdained whatever I suggested. Many the woeful slap Scratch absorbed for creeping too near Rusty's blanket or Dusty's burl.

During those lazy afternoon hours on the knoll in front of the cabin when even the sky was drowsy, and during the daily plunge in the lake or the Hautête, all three cubs invested what seemed to me an abnormal amount of time in playthings. Rusty wrestled and chewed for hours on a coffee can. When he took it swimming with him and when it sank below his diving ability, he would run to me bellowing like a calf until I rescued it. Fortunately, Dusty and Scratch played with objects that floated. Dusty rolled, boxed, and threw a large pine cone while Scratch pretended to defend an ordinary piece of firewood. I am totally ignorant as to what label zoologists would tag onto the cubs' affinity for toys. Their choice was as illogical to me as it was unpredictable.

I may be wrong, but I believe the bears gave more than a normal complement of happiness to each other. Their cocky joie de vivre was a reflection of the security they felt as a family. In my own mind, their toys represented an expression of individuality and personal integrity within their group. Scratch's block of wood was an immature outdoor copying of Rusty; without a toy he would have felt either conspicuous or left out. Indoors he chose to feign sleep in my lap, pretending to ignore the antics of the other two rather than cope with his own adventure in originality, although one barely perceptible slit of an eye followed every movement of his siblings.

On the fifteenth of September I stumbled onto paying gravel placer in a tributary ravine a hundred yards above Hautête Creek behind the cabin. The only hitch in the bonanza was the fact that the ravine was dry, and I had to pack the "diggin's" down to the creek in order to separate gold dust from detritus. I'd rather argue that I hadn't had sufficient time yet to build a sluice box than to admit I had deliberately procrastinated in order to spend more time with the cubs. They became bored with the routine of following me from the gravel pit to the creek and back, so they often loitered at the edge of the forest to perfect certain combinations of judo and karate for three and sometimes four participants. When I could stand it no longer, I dropped gold pan and shovel and joined in the fun. When I entered the contest, all three bears pocketed their personal grudges against each other, seized the opportunity to get even with me for suppressing indoor roughhousing, and put everything they had into a knock-down, drag-out, free-for-all that invariably ended in an evening with sewing kit, iodine, and adhesive tape. One hundred and eighty-five pounds of lightning-fast bear, distributed three ways, would have been a *lutte royale* for any medium-sized man.

Just as their feelings of affection and loyalty grew as the fall progressed, so did the intensity of their curiosity and interest increase in every detail of their sprawling wilderness surroundings. The natural wonders about them were mirrored in their daily enthusiasm to get going—provided it wasn't raining—and to explore every square foot of the Takla range with a gusto I cannot remember their having shown earlier. That enthusiasm was not concerned more than fifty percent with food, since they were interested in so many inedibles.

The success of this aspect of their development I attributed to the fact that there were no other people around to distract or confuse the simple activities I adhered to. Since my intentions from the beginning were to prepare the cubs for independence in an absolute wilderness, I studied every change in their behavior. Through determination to keep from domesticating them, I may have pushed them prematurely toward the rigorous, unbending wild world of competitive bears. I tried conscientiously to approach their problems of food, shelter, protection, self-assertion, play, and relationships with one another from the standpoint of bear, not human, criteria of behavior, indoor deportment excepting.

That the project was proceeding with some modicum of success was illustrated one morning while we were digging arrowrootlike rhizomes in a fermenting marsh. Without sounding an alarm, I allowed the approach of a big-footed, overgrown, two-year-old black bear who sneaked up on Scratch and nosed the cub over on his back. Despite a well-stocked aversion toward bear fights, I wanted to get a reaction. Their heads barely above the reeds, Rusty and Dusty stood up instantly to determine the cause of Scratch's howl. Within the same second or two they were at their brother's side exchanging uppercuts and fierce "vocabulary" with the older bear, rendering good accounts of themselves. The trio had almost chased the interloper away when suddenly they yielded to a much more bearlike proclivity, that of getting acquainted through the sense of smell. He really wasn't such a bad fellow after all; in fact, Dusty danced a bit in front of him. The two-year-old sniffed the air in my direction, watched me pick up and fondle the cubs, but regarded the act with trepidation. Although he walked with us for more than four miles, he didn't trust me closer to him than six feet. Back at the cabin, I refused to let him enter in spite of all his belly-crawling and disarming whines, since I wasn't sure what his two hundred pounds of outdoor manners might do to our well-ordered interior. The mistake of throwing him a salmon caused him to forage with us for the next seven days.

As the cubs played with the good-natured young boar, they demonstrated an astonishing sense of humor and capacity for planned tactics. When the older bear would lie down alongside the cabin for a snooze in the sun, Rusty would sneak up and slap him across the nose, a bear's most sensitive spot. As he uncoiled to seize his antagonist, Dusty and Scratch would bite the tendons above his hocks for tremendous, funny-bone shock effect. The boar would plunge forward and fall on his face every time the cubs pulled the trick. Even though the imps employed the same strategy time and again, he never learned that Rusty was baiting him into the trap. Unless you've seen bear cubs laugh, there is no way to describe the mirth they experienced at the expense of the young boar.

At the beginning of October, Rusty weighed eighty pounds; Dusty, seventy-five; and Scratch, the runt, about sixty. Nearly everything they ate went into growth instead of fat, but their appetites began tapering off following their frenetic gorging during September—nature's way of preparing them for hibernation.

I was removing some large, round, glacier-polished stones from the placer pit one day when I missed the cubs. The older bear had not been around for several days. At first I thought he might have returned to the cabin and that the cubs had run down the trail to romp with him. As a matter of habit, whenever they were not underfoot, I investigated. On this occasion they were not fifty feet away. Crouched in a semicircle, hackles raised, fangs bared, they silently faced the slow stalk of an adult wolverine, one of the most highly respected of medium-sized animals in the north woods because of his superior intelligence, formidable strength, brittle disposition, and tenacious will.

About the size of a large dachshund, the carcajou fixed his eyes on Scratch's throat. Advancing slowly, his head wove back and forth like the shuttle of a loom. He was feinting for an opening to dash in for a sudden kill. The bears seemed to recognize that a wolverine was a climber, so they made no attempt to tree. Besides, it was too late. Rusty and Dusty edged closer to Scratch, facing the enemy as a solid cheval-de-frise. It was their first life-and-death encounter since the muddy scrimmage with the dogs at Topley Landing. They were in good defensive position; but the wolverine was maneuvering in for a lightning thrust, a strategy in which his species is notoriously better equipped than his elected prey. The cubs seemed to know instinctively how to cope with the killer. At the last moment I lost my nerve to let them fight it out for educational reasons. When the intruder's back arched for the spring, I hit him behind the shoulders

with a shovel, throwing him off balance. He had
ignored or disdained my approach. Within half a
second of my attack, the code of the North was in-
voked. Like the coiled spring of a catapult, the cubs
released a furious demonstration of that terrible
warehouse of strength, speed, and desperate rage which
their kind so frequently seem unaware of possessing.
Tearing simultaneously into its soft underbelly, they
shredded the wolverine.

7

Surrender to Hibernation

The projected dry-gulch by the wolverine was no mere
chance encounter. The predator had no doubt stalked
his prey for days, as wolverines often do. The highly
unusual attack was another facet of life and death
under conditions of drought. Despite the showers immediately after the forest fire, it was a notably dry
summer. One or two rainless summers in north-central
British Columbia caused no concern; but when two
winters without snowpack were succeeded by two dry
summers, the entire population of delicately balanced
plant and animal life underwent upheaval.

One snappy morning we were scouting the depleted
range when the cubs stopped, raised their muzzles
toward the cloudless sky, sniffed, and turned to me
with quizzical expressions. The weather was about
to change. We had heard restive choruses of coyotes
the night before the atmospheric depression. The noisy
remaining bird flew aimlessly about as if crying the
news. The air was so light that morning that it gave
the forest shadows something of winter blue; not a
breath of wind stirred. The lake lay so still it looked

solid. By noon long, raveled mares' tails swept in from the west as forerunners of thickening nimbus. At sundown gentle rain began to enliven our atmosphere with the rich aroma of conifer duff which was imperceptible when the forest was dry. Late flocks of south-bound stormy petrels settled on the beach that night; but instead of their typical, sharp calls, often said to be the loneliest cry in nature, they whistled soft, drowsy harmonies that blended with the rain on the shakes—a total, moving sound pattern not unlike the muffled middle chords from a great pipe organ. With up-cupped ears and half-closed eyes, the cubs struggled against drowsiness to listen, because they knew I was listening to the strange rhythm.

After the showers our range deteriorated so rapidly, due to heavy frost, that I decided to risk leading the cubs farther afield for forage, which led to a discovery and, not so incidentally, to some feverish work before the snows set in. Quite by accident, I noticed a quantity of shot-size gold nuggets revolving in a solid-rock basin in a creek about two miles down the lake from the cabin. I hastened to move the sluice box.

With the backward-pointing fingers of the wooden baffles yielding about an ounce an hour, I was shoveling bedrock muck into the upper end of the trough one afternoon when I chanced to sight an embryonic drama in the making. The cubs were deployed to engage in a cooperative tactic of "surround and defeat." A delicious-looking animal they had never seen before was approaching with unprecedented temerity. Except for a pair of white stripes along his topside from the back of his head to the tip of his plumelike tail, he was solid black. Before I could warn the bears, they moved in for what appeared to their gleaming eye the easiest kind of phase-two operation. At this point the skunk arched his tail and broadcast 360 degrees of the most effective nonmuscular barrage in the animal kingdom. While the defeated cubs rolled in duff and grass, groaned, then raced for the lake, the skunk marched nonchalantly away as if nothing had happened. For two days and nights I fought a sleep-losing battle to keep the bears out of my sleeping bag. No amount of soap, water, and ashes reduced the memorable efficiency of the polecat's artillery. As long as the volatile, acid musk clung to their pelts, I was unable to get the cubs to eat. At length I was forced to use my precious quart of vinegar to eliminate the last traces of the potent scent.

They were wallowing in the smelly, blue mud of the creek where I was sluicing one morning shortly afterward when a mature racoon jumped from a tree and landed smack-dab on Rusty's upturned belly. The surprised cub bleated like a goat and batted the animal over to Dusty, who in turn flipped him like a tiddlywink to Scratch. The muddy bears were instantly upright in triangle formation, and I feared the unfortunate raccoon would be torn to shreds before I could reach the scene, or worse, that one of the bears—remembering my rule of sharing—might suddenly flip him into my arms. An agitated raccoon, like an infuriated lynx, is easier to receive than to turn loose. This bushy-tailed fellow, a prime boar, was both agitated and infuriated.

When I arrived, the grinning bears had closed any avenue through which the captive might hope to escape. They seemed rather to admire the plucky, outnumbered, outleagued gladiator who was standing upright in the center of the triangle, loudly and belligerently daring the cubs to attempt any further indignities. Rusty sensed that I was about to liberate their prisoner, so he rushed in for one final cuff which rolled the unhappy raccoon like a bowling ball down the creek bed. I could have sworn I observed three sets of lifted eyebrows during the lecture I delivered on cruelty to dumb animals.

Long after the last sockeye and chinook had spawned in Hautête Creek, big rainbow trout moved in from the lake to establish their redds in smooth gravel on the wake side of boulders. They were meticulously careful not to disturb salmon redds already on the bottoms of the same pools and eddies. Unlike most salmon species, sockeye and chinook spawn only in streams which are lake tributaries. The lake acts as a rearing pond for a year before the fry swim downstream to the rigors of ocean life.

At the time the trout began spawning, a yearling otter appeared on the left bank for some open-and-shut fishing. The bears watched the strange creature fill up on fish, then crawl halfway up the bank to lie in the sun. They whined for permission to swim the creek, but I forbade it on the grounds that it might encourage wandering; besides, I didn't want that otter hurt. On the following day the happy vagabond showed up on our bank. The cubs raced over toward him but were no match for the graceful aquatic animal, who tried to entice them into the water with him.

When he entered the lake that afternoon while the cubs were bathing, I saw all three bears lay their ears back as they always did when about to engage in mischief. Through binoculars I studied the scene from the cabin porch as the otter joined them. Keeping barely out of reach, but giving the cubs competition they had not yet known, the otter slithered in and out among them until they lost interest after an hour's frustrating attempts to nail the crafty swimmer. The next day they waded into shallow water and assumed the strategy of ignoring him. Like poodles, seals, and chimpanzees, performing otters can't bear to remain disregarded. His passes became carelessly close. What he wanted, of course, was a playmate or two, someone to slide down the banks with, someone to romp in the water with. The bears had no way of interpreting his intentions. To them he was an impertinent pest. With one sudden powerful swipe of his right arm, Rusty uppercut the otter under the chin and broke the little fellow's neck.

The bears hung their heads in what I hoped was genuine remorse as they followed me to a little rise behind the toolshed where I buried the unfortunate victim—after removing his valuable pelt.

Rusty, like the other two, had lost all fear of punishment, because I have never punished them. When he drooped in shame at the tragedy and looked up appealingly, with a calflike expression, it was through fear of disapproval, rather than some physical bastinado. He realized I was unhappy about the otter's death not through any outward remonstrance, but through the seriousness of my insinuating stare. Since the swat had been the culmination of the well-planned snub, we couldn't regard the incident as an accident; therefore, I felt he'd learn more by stewing for a while in the juice of his own conscience before I rescued him. Distasteful as such situations inevitably were, he chose to suffer my abusive scowls rather than attempt to bribe me with overt displays of affection like those Dusty and Scratch had used in similar circumstances.

The more the chills of October frosted the alders, aspens, and meadows, the more difficult foraging became. There were days when I was unable to clean the baffles in the sluice box because it was too late when I returned with the bears. We had made our way one morning through brush along the beach about four miles below the cabin, when the cubs' sensitive noses ferreted out the freshly killed carcass of a large buck deer. By claw marks on the back and the chewed throat, I knew the brush-concealed kill was the property of a cougar. The hungry bears began stripping the leg and loin muscles for their first serious feast on red meat. By standing on the ground, they now mustered sufficient strength to reach across the carcass, lean against it on one elbow, and rip the hide with the other paw.

A bit of falling bark directed my attention up the fir against which I sat while the cubs ate. Watching every move we made from fifty feet directly overhead, tail swaying back and forth, a full-grown tom lion sat sharpening his claws against the branch to which he nervously clung. In panic I came near shouting, "Tree!" That could have been the end of Rusty, Dusty, and Scratch—and Leslie! Fortunately the cougar stayed put until the extravagantly gorged cubs abandoned the carcass.

By mid-October I gave up for that year further efforts to earn a living panning gold. The water temperature had dropped to thirty-eight degrees, for one thing; and for another, it took most of ten daylight hours every day to explore fallen logs, rocks, dried-out meadows, and small rodent tunnels to show the cubs where they might find food in the season of most stringent scarcity. Fortunately rainbow and Dolly Varden trout rose for gray gnat and hackle lures, while big, blubbery char and sucker took helgrammites on the bottom of the lake fifty yards beyond the mouth of Hautête Creek. The cubs were always excited when I took them fishing in the canoe. There each would sit and pound or gnaw the gunwale while awaiting his turn for a fish. When they considered themselves full, they would plop over the side and swim ashore. The world's most avid sightseers, they never jumped out as long as I kept moving; but they preferred a long swim in ice water to sitting in a drafty canoe once their hunger was satisfied.

Toward the middle of the month, I had smoked three hundred pounds of fish for the food cache. Increasing wind and millions of autumn leaves constantly hitting the choppy water, however, soon made fishing impractical.

The twentieth day of October marked the beginning of a full week of snow and sleet both night and day. Although the cubs were heavy and well filled out, they had not stored enough fat to carry them through a lengthy hibernation. Even small hibernators in the Takla Lake region didn't go to sleep until November; therefore, I couldn't expect the bears to stop eating entirely before Thanksgiving. During the first three days of the storm there was enough rain mixed with the snow to melt most of it, so we could still travel about; but if I had thought feeding the bears *before* the freeze was difficult, I had to redefine the adjective after the surface of our world lay two and three feet beneath the level where we walked.

In their autumn-thickened, dark-brown pelage, the cubs were beautiful against the pure white snow. Like young children, they seized every opportunity to romp and roll in the dry, white powder after one cautious, initial sortie. Scratch was the only ticklish cub of the trio, so much so that he couldn't stand to lick the bottoms of his own feet until he was a year old. Each time he left the warm cabin, the snow tickled his naked soles for about half an hour. For relief he would jump like a bullfrog and cling to the trunks of trees while he bawled for Rusty and Dusty to wait for him.

In most respects I was pleased with the way in which they had grown into their own wild corner of the bush. They divided their world into three comfortable categories: fun, food, and sleep. I was never able to determine which of the three was most important to them from their standpoint. And though the snow eclipsed the probability of further balanced diets for that season, it provided a new dimension in fun and sleep.

When I tired of my shelf of winter reading material, there were long hours to ponder my following year's responsibility to the bears. There was also the austere fact that escape was now unalterably blocked until late March when Red Fern and my landlord could get in. I hoped to pan enough gold to stay at least beyond the cubs' second year. At that time they would be independent. The early snow and continuing appetites drove me to construct a bow, to fletch a dozen straight willow shoots, and to file out some sharp steel arrowheads in order to feed the cubs for another couple of weeks. Once again I regretted the day I had turned down Red Fern's offer of the loan of his 30-30, for now I should have to hunt in a primitive manner far more repulsive to me than rifle hunting.

I was practicing my archery against targets half the size of a deer's chest one afternoon, when I was distracted by a pack of howling, baying wolves down by the beach. Rushing around the cabin, I saw six adult wolves leaping at the bleeding throat of a bellowing bull moose. No pack of *twenty* wolves would take on a prime bull unless the animal was a victim of a gunshot wound from the Babine or Stuart Lake districts, where hunters drove in by automobile and took motorboats up into moose country. Each year many victims of poor shooting limped or crawled away to die sooner or later. It depended upon the time it took the wolves to keep them moving—and therefore bleeding—until they dropped to their knees from exhaustion and loss of blood. At that time the predators closed with their victim.

Red Fern once told me that it was uncanny the way the wolves moved in each year when the hunting season began. He avowed that more game was wounded and lost annually than was actually felled and taken home by the hunters.

I didn't wait for the wolves to eat their fill or for neighboring coyotes, foxes, bears, lynxes, lions, and a bevy of small predators to follow the moose's trail of blood. Locking the howling, squealing, objecting cubs inside the cabin and seizing saw and butcher knife, I headed for the dead moose with an old toboggan I had repaired earlier. My satisfaction lay in the irony of the tragedy: I would not be forced to hunt with bow and arrow. Chasing the timber wolves away each trip by throwing rocks at them at point-blank range, I carved and sawed out some five hundred pounds of lean meat which I hung to freeze that night beneath the platform of the food cache.

For the four days and nights it took for the frozen carcass to disappear as if it had never been there, I did not allow the cubs one single meal at the site for fear of attack by the unusual number of nocturnal predators lurking nearby. Night prowlers became day prowlers when a carcass lay about. Lions, grizzlies, and wolves lost interest when the viscera and large muscles had been consumed. Coyotes, foxes, badgers, and lynxes gnawed the frozen bones. Black bears, minks, rats, mice, and raccoons carried away the final traces. I hung the magnificent rack above the fireplace.

Other gifts of the north woods included the wonderful sounds and smells of early winter. Except for the occasional ditties of ouzels and snowbirds or the thumping cackle of a ptarmigan, the forest was no longer the land of birdsong it had been before the September migrations; yet new melodies surged forth. Timber wolves, for instance, sang as they had never sung before the snow. Moose and elk trumpeted oftener. The silent red fox became the chatterbox of the woods. Sounds of inanimate origin also took on new meaning: the crash of a squaw wood branch heavy with snow, the grumble of a distant avalanche. Before winter I had never noticed the slapping of the whirlpool where Hautête Creek spun into the lake. These were the early winter sounds—spaced with time for contemplation in between—which one could expect to hear when the wind stuttered down to a whisper in the pine needles.

By far the most imposing personality of the northern winter was the wind. From the frozen polar sea, the vagrant blizzards howled across the Klondike and could freeze a man in his tracks. A north-moving chinook could then roll in from the Pacific side within an hour or so and thaw him out. Either wind could whistle fascinating little bars at sundown or shriek blood-curdling, auditory illusions of foulest murder around darkest midnight. It wasn't the notorious stillness of the Canadian bush that gave me the feeling of loneliness. It was the wind that on more than one occasion convinced me that I was an outcast, a derelict abandoned, expelled, and exiled.

As if to complement the miracles of sight and sound, winter brought a fresh newness of smell to the air: an ozone-like cleanliness to the norther and salty lilt to the warm chinook. Both winds seemed to entice entirely different, latent fragrances from balsam pitch and needle honey. The wet, fishy smells of lake and stream simply vanished with the freeze.

Almost daily the cubs showed less enthusiasm for long hikes. After a short romp in the snow they wanted to return indoors for hearthside snoozes. By the middle of November their appetites tapered off almost to zero. Although the bears were anything but fat, their growth rate during the autumn had been so rapid that I was forced to alter our sleeping arrangements. The four of us could no longer occupy one bed with comfort. Since the cubs' hibernation would be only partial in that they could awaken at any time, I built a small cabinlike structure in one corner of the big room where they could sleep undisturbed for as long as they liked. Rusty and Dusty took to the idea at once and curled up together on blankets which I stuffed into the new quarters. I gave in to Scratch's pleas to remain my bedfellow at least for the time being.

Ordinarily the hibernation of black bears is controlled by weather, particularly by depth of snow which prevents foraging and to some extent locomotion. They may go into deep sleep as early as September or may defer it until late January, depending upon the conditions of a given winter. They will, however, awaken and move about during every thaw, seeking a small amount of water but no food, until late March or early April.

Rusty and Dusty stopped eating and fell asleep on the eighteenth of November, which was the day the lake began to freeze with startling reports like shotgun fire. Scratch continued to sit with me before the fire of an evening for another week and munch without gusto small bits of broiled moose or smoked trout. After a bowel movement on the twenty-fifth of November, he returned to the cabin and nosed his way in with Rusty and Dusty. The latter two shifted positions in the hibernation shelter to welcome their brother for the lengthy nap.

Between the first and fifteenth of December I never left the cabin for more than half an hour at a time. Only for the briefest periods did it stop snowing, and the long red thermometer by the door often read forty-five degrees below zero. According to popular misconception, it was supposed to stop snowing when the temperature became too cold. It never got that cold in the lake country! Every second day I shoveled snowdrifts away from the food cache; otherwise small animals might have gnawed their way in. I couldn't allow the snow to pile up above the windows because it was too dark inside for reading even by candlelight. Dull sunrise—somewhere above the snow clouds—was not before 9:30 A.M. and sunset was around 2:30 P.M. I pampered my claustrophobia by keeping the porch clear, by opening the storm shutters every morning, and by shoveling as much snow as possible away from the outside walls. By the end of the storm the cabin was sitting at the bottom of a snow well, but my peace of mind made it worth the effort. More for exercise than for convenience, I kept a ten-foot-wide trench open between the cabin and the lake.

The morning of the fifteenth broke with such brilliance that I rushed out before breakfast to behold the shining white wonderland of icicles, windrowed drifts, indigo sky, and dark trees. In the violently glaring sheen of early sunlight, the forest as such disappeared due to an exaggerated dimension presented by the strong contrast of light and shadow: each tree, sprouting from its own snow well, stood out for the first time as a friendly individual; and I was never again—regardless of season—able to look out there and see a forest.

The solitary figure of a man—a very tall, slender man, lithe as a panther—moved with Indian cadence on snowshoes across the frozen lake. A ten-foot breath-cloud followed him as he hurried directly toward my cabin.

8

Larch of the North Woods

*Through binoculars, I watched the rhythmic up-and-*down winking of the Indian's showshoes as he walked, but I could not wait in the freezing wind for him to cross the flat miles of Takla Lake. Despite his swiftly springing gait, he'd be cold when he arrived and would appreciate a roaring five and hot coffee. I purposely kept the cabin temperature much below what was humanly comfortable, because every time I stoked the fire too heavily the bears would wake up, crawl out, and stumble stupidly around the room. They never complained at the disturbance; rather they seemed to welcome the opportunity to clasp their arms around my waist and lick my hands as if *I* had been the absentee. They learned that such outward displays of affection meant that their chins and bellies would be scratched before I opened the door to admit enough winter to send them back into hibernation.

When I heard the leathery creak of snow as the Indian entered the trench between the lake and the cabin, I went out to meet him. The Beaver tribe was famous for the handsomest Indians in North America, and this fellow, from what I could see of his six-foot frame beneath his wolfskin parka, hood, and quilted trousers, was one of the most strikingly attractive of the tribe. There was a firm-footed spring about his swinging walk in high-cut moose moccasins made with the hair on the insides. He removed his hood and a pair of thin-slitted wooden eye masks.

"I'm Larch A-Tas-Ka-Nay. I believe you know my father." We removed our elbow-length gauntlets and shook hands. "I read the note you left in my cabin, but I couldn't get over until the lake froze solid."

When he grinned, a breath-cloud momentarily concealed his beaming face.

"Come on in, Larch, and let's get acquainted since we're going to be neighbors for the winter. Coffee's ready. Have you had breakfast?"

"Long ago, but the wind has bedeviled me with the coffee for the last two miles. Are the bears in hibernation?"

"Uh-huh. You know about the bears?"

"Everybody in Topley Landing still laughs about Rusty, Dusty, and Scratch."

"Yes, they're in and out of hibernation. I don't know what their reaction will be. Let's find out."

When I removed the heavy, quarter-sawed lid, the bears awoke slowly, yawned, stretched, and made a beeline for Larch. Before they would allow him to touch them, they stood on their hind legs and walked around and around him sniffing, especially the long wolfskin jacket. When he removed the garment and his moccasins, they studied him from head to foot, cooing first to me then to one another. The personable Indian's friendly smile and easy speech, coupled with an understanding of animals that set him apart even among Indians, soon had the cubs climbing all over him as he sat on the hearth and tried to drink his coffee. I explained why I had the animals and that I was attempting to raise them as wild as possible so they could enjoy a normal life in their own habitat and retain pleasant memories of people provided they could lose an early recollection.

"Your purposes are now well-known to the Indians, but if these bears saw their mother killed by men, they won't forget it," he assured me. "Bears are about as intelligent as people, and more discreet. They remember and like and hate on an individual basis." There was an underlying note of bitterness in the analogy.

Larch's speech reflected meditation, and the inflections of his voice were as soft as the shadows beneath the big pines where he dwelt. It was difficult to picture him as a trapper.

"I'm twenty-seven years old," he said. "I have trapped for seven winters. Filthy business. I despise it. We're all kinda looking forward to the time when there'll be other ways an Indian can make a living in British Columbia in the winter. I'll miss the nights and days of solitude, though, on Takla Lake, where a man can think in absolute silence. I don't believe I could really think straight in a city."

"Any further news of this region becoming a provincial park?"

"The newspapers are full of it, but the lumber combines, trappers, hunting guides, and sporting goods outfitters are against it. The Hudson's Bay Company's still uncommitted. What they decide may swing it one way or another. They grease the wheels up here, you know.

"Personally I don't want to see it become a park

with roads and gas fumes and motels and beer cans. But a game and timer reserve, yes."

"How did you come in, and when?" I asked.

"Trucked the boat and outboard to Fort Fraser. Took the Nechako River to the Stuart. Came up the Stuart to Fort Saint James. Bought my supplies there, then followed Stuart Lake to Middle River, Trembleur Lake, back to Middle River, then into Takla. Got in just before the freeze. Dad and Red Fern will come in the same way when they bring your supplies this spring."

"Tell me, Larch," I began with caution, which Larch sensed and smiled at, "where did you go to school?"

"I suppose I don't talk much like an Indian anymore. My parents sent me first to Vandlerhoof, then to Prince George, where I won a scholarship to Vancouver. Once out of school, I went to work for the lumber company like every other Indian. Began winter trapping because of the annual layoff from November to May."

Both his palms showed heavy callouses, but those on his right hand were all out of proportion to those on his left, and his right biceps was developed far beyond his left—all from the way loggers and fallers grip ax, saw, and peavey.

After bringing Larch up to date on the events of the summer and autumn, I asked about his future, since he planned to give up trapping. His answer was surprising.

"An Indian can't plan too much for the future," he said, "so I enjoy the past and am damned careful with the present."

As Larch continued to speak about himself and his people, the cubs nestled up close to him and stared at his face as if trying to comprehend his softly enunciated words. It may have been a demonstration of that sixth sense animals are supposed to have which lets them know whom they can trust and whom they cannot.

"Before lunch let's hike up through the forest and drop back by way of the beach. The bears can come along for exercise up and down a few trunks," I suggested.

They ate a considerable amount of snow but refused all food that Larch and I offered them.

During our lengthy afternoon conversation, we let the fire die down to the point where the cubs sought their own company inside the hibernation shelter near the door. When I mentioned the catastrophe of the Babine forest fire, Larch assured me that the Indians did not consider forest fires cataclysmic.

"We recognize," he said, "that there are immediate tragedies; but see what happened to your robin in the talons of the duck hawk."

"The logic of your argument eludes me, Larch!"

He smiled as he put his hand on my shoulder and explained, "My friend, the area burned over now becomes dynamic grassland and brushland for many years. Grass supports a larger animal population than forest duff. For Indians hunting meat and hides, open land means abundance." Never taking his eyes from mine, he paused to let the idea sink in before proceeding.

I had to acknowledge that there was some advantage from the standpoint of the Indians. He reemphasized the fact that the sterile, shady forest floor produced nothing in the way of food which could support an ungulate. There were no cities to be flooded when the snow melted; stream pollution from rapid runoff from the ravished hills would settle out in the lakes. Trout, salmon, and grayling, according to Larch, would be set back for but two spawns.

"The lumbering combines simply shift their operations slightly. Up here there is always more timber," he declared. "When I was a child, it was such fun to follow my father and other members of the tribe during early fall when they made a feast of controlled burning! Indians never burned big timber. Their purpose was to improve the range. The mills had laws passed to stop us from all burning, but our Thunder God took over and now destroys a vast acreage of big timber. Since the Indians are not allowed to burn the understory, it has become dense enough to ignite the big trees once it is set by lightning."

I couldn't gainsay the ancient lore.

"But what of the birds?" I asked.

"There are never more than two or three pairs of nesting birds per forest acre; just seems as there are more because of the males' songs. On bushland— depending on food supply—there's often one or more nests in every bush. The only serious food competition's between members of the same species; so when a bush contains three nests, they'll all belong to different kinds of birds with different food requirements.

"In the balanced communities of forest as well as grassland, each species serves as a specialist designed by the Creator for a specific purpose. The strongest, fastest, and most intelligent reach old age. The first to tire or weaken is first to fall victim to a predator or disease. Gitchy-Manitou's apparent indifference toward the individual is often misinterpreted by those who cannot see beyond certain immediacies to the great, moving, overall plan of life.

"Considering the food chain alone," Larch continued, "no northern forest can support a large population of animals. The insect feeds upon the leaves of grassland. The spider catches the insect. The wasp paralyzes the spider and feeds it to her young. The phoebe catches the wasp; the hawk takes the phoebe. The night-prowling weasel ambushes the hawk; the wolverine, the weasel; the wolf, the wolverine; man, the wolf; and the insect again carries a disease that is fatal to man. Such a complicated cycle cannot possibly reach completion in the shade and leaf mold of the forest floor.

"And if the forest community's really balanced," the young man went on, "we must keep a forest cover over a large portion of the earth's surface. Forest soil doesn't freeze because of the carpet of duff and snow. Forest shade slows down melting and runoff in the spring. Forests certainly provide a haven for the pursued. They also supply man with a number of essentials besides lumber—even if such essentials are intrinsic and can't be entered on the debit side of a cash ledger."

We continued our discussions until far into the night, then robbed the bears of their extra blankets to make a pallet for Larch in front of the hearth. At my insistence he remained until the following afternoon, at which time he had to begin his trapline rounds, a three-day trip by toboggan which led all the way over the Pacific Divide of the Hogem Range of the Ominecas to Purvis Lake. When I gave him the skin of the otter, he said he could buy more than two months' supplies with the proceeds of that one valuable pelt. I agreed to join him upon his return and accompany him frequently along the entire route if the bears remained in deep slumber.

Maintaining an interior temperature of about fifty-five degrees except during the preparation of my two meals a day, I would try to keep the cubs asleep until I could get away. Without glowing logs, of course, the temperature inside would drop to ten or fifteen degrees below zero and stay there. My wards would not budge until I returned. Larch assured me that all the usual Indian signs pointed toward ten days of cold sunshine.

I'll never forget the deep warmth and sincere smile of this fellow as I trudged up to his door where he welcomed me with gentle, softly spoken words typical of the north woods Beaver, and so unlike the expressions of welcome anywhere else on earth. I have often heard Indians say, "My land breathes an air more fragrant and pure because you are here!" or "The Sun God smiles more brightly, even the trees are greener, the snow glistens with new brilliance where you have stepped!" Anywhere else on this continent such expressions would be tagged gross exaggerations and insincere poppycock, but these Beaver people said nothing unless they meant it.

At first I was chagrined at having packed a moose loin strip into the Trapper Nelson and back-toted it five miles through fluffy snow. It so happened that Larch had killed a moose for trapline bait as well as for his own use. A half ton of red meat hung in his food cache, but he assuaged my embarrassment by stating that his kill was neither as well-bled nor as aged as mine. We skewered the strip and broiled it over aspen charcoal in the fireplace where potatoes were baking as a special treat, since the black behemoth had gobbled down all of mine when I up-ended in the Hautête Creek rapids.

Larch and I shared the traces of the toboggan by means of a double breast harness which we rigged to chest-tump the supplies, tools, gear, and sleeping bags up the canyon some fifteen miles to the summit of the Fraser watershed. The Pacific Divide—otherwise known as the Continental Divide—lay at the head of a wide col that had no name on any map. Our destination was Purvis Lake, about ten miles into the Mackenzie or Arctic watershed. Fortunately, Larch had already tree-blazed a trail of sorts except where he had purposely obliterated any traces of human presence in the vicinity of his traps.

On the first day out we reached within a mile of the Divide because so few of the traps held fur bearers or had been sprung. With a .22 rifle Larch killed two red foxes, a white weasel, and a pine marten all of which he case-skinned, slipping the pelt over U-shaped willow branches for stretching, fleshing, and drying after the spring thaw. That evening we dug into the snow at the mouth of a cabin-sized cave, but we had to push on because of two hibernating grizzlies inside. They did not awaken, but they might have had we started a fire; and a .22 wouldn't stop a grizzly. Half a mile farther on we dug out a fine shelter at the base of a cliff, constructed a lean-to of hemlock and lodgepole branches, and stoked a reflector fire against the rocks which kept us warm all night. Larch slept as if he were embalmed, but my thoughts were of Rusty, Dusty, and Scratch. Not to mention my sore muscles, all sorts of horrible possibilities crept in to preclude sleep.

Once over the Divide, Larch accumulated six more pelts. I didn't think too much at the time about each animal's torture of pain, cold, and personal tragedy,

possibly because of my own continuous efforts to keep
from freezing. By lifting first one foot, then the other,
I did a sort of danse macabre around the shiny,
skinned carcasses. Another thing that made the sinister business more bearable was the fact that five out of
the six animals had frozen before we arrived, so I was
spared those last looks of terror before Larch's coup
de grace.

A steady Arctic wind got up near dark, which then
came at perhaps three o'clock at that latitude. We
never carried any form of time machine in the lake
country. Knowing the exact time of day seemed to
distract from the fun we got out of living as if it were
a thousand years ago. Larch said the temperature had
dropped to about fifty below zero. Every half hour
we broke icicles from the fronts of our parka hoods,
the result of breath condensation. During the day, our
wooden eye masks, with slits you couldn't push a two-
bit piece through, would frost over about once an hour,
but we had to keep them on for fear of snow blindness
or frostbitten eyelids. Keeping dry meant keeping
warm, thus we always made a practice of stopping
when we began to perspire. Damp undergarments could
be most uncomfortable—even a health menace if they
began to freeze.

On the shore of Purvis Lake we shoveled the snow
away from the door of a cabin that Larch had repaired,
ratproofed, and furnished many years before. The
ancient structure, without wooden floor or windows,
had been built by sourdoughs during the Nation Lakes-
Omineca gold rush in the 1870's. Whoever built
it knew his business, because Larch declared that no
matter how high the snow drifted elsewhere—sometimes
up to seventy or one hundred feet—he had never seen
it pile up more than halfway to the overhang of this
cabin, including what slid off the steep-pitched,
flagstone-slab roof. Intending to sleep twelve men on
tiered bunks along the sides, the builder had erected
a high platform Swedish fireplace that occupied the
entire end of the cabin opposite the door; and although
this consumed an enormous amount of wood, it had
certain practical aspects when it came to preparing

meals commensurate with northern work and appetites. Once properly stacked, fired, and coaled, with the door open just a sliver—then restacked and finally dampered by closing the door—the great fireplace would heat the tiers of beds all night and leave ample coals for breakfasts of oatmeal porridge, sowbelly, pemmican, johnnycakes, and black tea.

During the morning we hiked to the crest of a rocky ridge which opened to the southeast of Purvis Lake and afforded an unlimited view. The ninety-mile chain of Nation Lakes lay backdropped near the center of the frozen basin by the cloudlike Mount Nation. The temperature in the open sunlight reached nearly seventy degrees, while in the shade of the hemlocks twenty feet away, the clutch of winter held firm at thirty below. After Larch pointed out all the headwater tributaries of the Nation River known to contain placer gold, we discussed plans to prospect the region soon after the arrival of supplies in spring. The yearling bears would encounter no difficulties in satisfying their expanding appetites on the watershed of the Nation drainage system. It was a 10,000-square-mile realm of mountain peaks, Arctic tundra, springy muskeg, meadows, streams, lakes, beech savannahs, and solidly forested hillsides and canyons—10,000 square miles landlocked and sealed apart from the rest of the Dominion where a bear might spend his entire anticipated quarter of a century without ever hearing the sound of steel trap or firearm. Larch and I exchanged a lengthy glance which expressed more than words.

"I just might make the move," I said.

"The only trouble would be supplies," he pointed out. "However, if you like, I'll teach you how to live off this country."

With food to spare, we spent another night in the Purvis Lake cabin before making the steep, ten-mile ascent back to where the cliffs of the Divide faced west. Once on the Takla Lake side, we shifted positions frequently: one man pulled the toboggan while the other held it off the lead's heels while we were on steep coulees along the fifteen miles of descending canyon.

On treeless drops we both rode the toboggan until
our eyeballs ached as they did when we ate snow too
rapidly. There were no catches along the trapline, so
we reached Larch's cabin on Takla Lake before
dark.

The days between Christmas and March seemed
to mesh into months before my friend and I were aware
of their passing. We were together most of those days.
If the cubs knew of my having stepped out on them—
occasionally for as much as a week at a time—they
never raised an eyelid when I returned. In the space
of nine weeks they awakened and emerged from their
shelter but twice: once to sit and lean against Larch
A-Tas-Ka-Nay near the hearth and once to go outside
just long enough to urinate. They had evacuated their
bowels before hibernation.

During February there was almost no reason to in-
spect the traplines oftener than twice, since most of
the fur bearers had been taken for the season or had
migrated. Larch's permit did not allow him to set
his traps in other canyons, because each licensed
trapper had signed a government affidavit to trap only
within a specifically registered area. Infringement by
poachers and violation of assigned territories had
generated many fierce trapper wars, in which the Royal
Canadian Mounted Police figured dramatically.

Each time the wind blew the snow off the surface
of the lake, we chopped holes in the ice through which
we fished for rainbow and Dolly Varden trout, using
chunks of moose meat for bait. When we didn't feel
up to a fish fry and there were no immediate pressures
of weather, we hiked over the limitless hills and cols
on both sides of our sparkling, white domain to count
returning moose, elk, deer, wolves, and cougars. In
the uplands along the Divide we saw herds of white
Dall's sheep, the most regal animals in America.

"Think what it would be like to get through the
underbrush and devil's claw for all the miles we've
covered on the snow," Larch often repeated, recalling
the difficulty with which one travels in summer through
a Canadian forest without trails.

During the storms of late February and early March,

when we were unable to hike, we made furniture for the two cabins and "luxury gadgets" like bread boards, clothes baskets, and boot racks. We tooled the dry alder and aspen wood entirely by hand. When we ran out of things to build, we dressed down finish lumber for future projects. The bears paid no attention to the hammering, planing, and sawing. The one piece of civilized furniture I missed most was a chest of drawers; so we devoted one entire storm to that extravagance. I got my chest, a handsome piece by any standard of north woods furnishings. In addition to his skill as a woodsman, Larch was an accomplished craftsman, an artisan with hammer, saw, plane, and chisel.

There was so much more pleasant work to do than there were hours in which to do it! "Industry, like happiness," Larch said one day, "is an educated attitude."

We weren't always inclined to noble labor. There were times when we just sat staring at fire patterns and pondering the weighty issues of life after death, predestination, or original sin. On more than one occasion we debated the physical merits and moral *de*merits of somebody's obscure suggestion that we import a couple of Fort Saint James squaws to help with all that work that seemed to accumulate during the hibernation season.

Cursing the depth of the snow, the impossible distance to Fort Saint James of a winter, and my sworn vow of responsibility to the bears, we would then invariably dip too deeply into our precious and religiously rationed supply of Meyers black Jamaica rum. On the following day Larch saw to it that we either built something unnecessarily complicated or shoveled an inordinate amount of snow.

9

Awakening Yearlings

Although wispy frost vapor still veiled the lower halves of trees and shrubs at dawn, winter's icy bondage seemed on the break after the equinox. Between nine and ten o'clock of a clear evening, the lights of the aurora borealis staggered across the sky like drunken rainbows. Generally accompanying the lashing spectrum was a motorlike noise of electricity, sometimes more of a crackling static like that produced by rubbing the back of a furry animal on a dry day. Almost as strange as the dancing lights themselves, the stillness of all animal life during the heavenly display seemed to indicate either fear or wonder at the brilliant spectacle. The temperature always moderated to forty above zero after the aurora. Precipitation on cloudy mornings then fell in the form of rain instead of snow.

The bears had stirred, turned, whined, and scratched often without actually emerging during the last two weeks of March. On Good Friday evening Rusty crawled through the shelter door, yawned half a dozen times, sat down in front of my chair, and leaned back against my knees. When he nuzzled my hand for a head scratching, I decided he must be fully awake. How he had grown! His restlessness was explained the following day by the arrival of a southwesterly chinook that blew in on that Easter Sunday. With premature thawing, icicles dripped, snapped, and fell throughout the night. Rumbling like distant thunder, snow cornices and ice gables avalanched down the faces of Omineca cliffs.

Dusty and Scratch looked up with heavy eyelids

and a snarl when I lifted the top of the shelter for a peep inside. They declined an invitation to come and sit by the fire with Rusty and me.

On the heels of the early thaw, a blizzard—called a norther up here—swooped down from the polar sea and pushed back the air wall of warm chinook. Giant air pools of dense, gelid fog swirled about for two days, refreezing the landscape, causing trees to burst with the report of a muffled cannon, and visiting all sorts of hardships upon an awakening animal population. Four or five times during the chinook I heard long, crunching groans along the lakeshore; but the blizzard refroze the breaking ice. Larch had predicted the Easter disturbance, and we were unable to visit again until the ice broke for good.

Because of the long, southern body of the Y-shaped lake, and because I lived on one side and Larch on the other where the two arms came together, there were but two ways to cross: one was by ice when the lake was frozen over, and the other was by boat. Neither of us dared risk it across just before the breakup. He had often said, "Don't start across after you hear the first crunch. Death in ice water is painfully slow, but certain." So we had to wait until late April for the full thaw before we could begin paddling back and forth across the five-mile channel.

After seven warm days, life returned to budland. By day the April singing of hermit thrushes, bluebirds, and waxwings first proclaimed squatters' rights on southern exposures where some of the deep drifts had melted; and by night that most pleasant of all evening sounds, the song of the great horned owl, whose nesting eagerness had begun in February, blended with the mating calls of wolves and coyotes. Crickets and frogs came out of hibernation and in their turn sang double time, it seemed, to make up for all those months of inactivity. Larch declared they sang less in spring than in summer, and that my ears were deceiving me because they had grown accustomed to the profound silence of winter.

I believe it was the first of May when I paddled and poled my way across the lake through dark-green shifting aisles between the melting masses of icebergs that could have drifted together with sufficient force either to crush the canoe—and man and bears—or to throw the vessel completely out of the water. I was never so glad to reach the other shore.

"I was going to row the skiff over to your side tomorrow," Larch shouted as he ran down to the beach to catch the bow painter and pull us ashore. "I can't expect Red Fern and Dad for another ten days. Too damned much ice piling up at the lower end. The Middle River's blocked to beat hell. How are your supplies?"

"Low! We're all starving to death! That's why we came over to leech a meal. What have you been doing?"

"Been fleshing hides and pulling in the traps. Glad to say I didn't lose any this winter."

Losing a trap told a mute story of horror worse than any other phase of the despicable industry.

The yearling bears were all over Larch, and Scratch refused to leave him even to forage with Rusty and Dusty in the interesting canyon behind the cabin.

"They grew during hibernation," Larch observed. "They're in excellent shape. Forty-eight teeth now to match their bigger appetites—but they won't eat much of anything for a while because their guts collapse during hibernation—just grass, roots, and a few lodgepole buds. Don't worry about it. If you're long on smoked salmon, give 'em each half a pound a day."

"They'll never be able to get along this year on last year's range," I said as we entered the cabin for coffee and raisins. Scratch joined us.

"Mayn't I offer some very ancient Indian advice, Bob?" he asked with his usual, mischievous eye-twinkle. "Within the month you'll not be able to follow those bears for more than half a day. So let 'em forage for themselves. They'll stay together, and they'll always come home, just like a dog. Stop worryin' about 'em now if you want 'em to be able to get along on their own. Nature's hourglass is running out on your time with those bears, so let's face it. Dammit, Bob, I had to tell you that!"

"That brings up my alternative, Larch," I said. "All winter long the notion has stuck in my craw to transport them to the zoo in Vancouver. If this region is not protected against hunting . . ."

"No wild animal is better off in a cage unless he's born in one. That's for damned sure."

I knew he spoke the truth, and sooner or later I'd have to face the inevitable.

"That's been my dilemma."

The snow was deep where winter still clung tenaciously to northern exposures, but ice blocks along the river soon melted and floated away, resembling a flood of cotton bolls. The throat of the lake cleared to permit Red Fern and the elder A-Tas-Ka-Nay to come in. I was about to leave with the bears for a long morning forage when the sound of an outboard motor attracted and held my attention. The boat whined across the lake. Rushing back to the cabin, I got the binoculars to study the three men aboard. They were Larch, his father, and Red Fern. The long Hudson's Bay bateau was piled high with cardboard cartons filled with half a year's supplies.

"I can't believe these scrawny varmints were ever the cubs that raised so much hell in Topley Landing," Red Fern said as we began hauling boxes to the cabin.

"I am old and shall not be needing this cabin anymore, Bob," said Peter A-Tas-Ka-Nay after scrutinizing the work Larch and I had done on it. "You can live here in peace with your wild people. We spent last night with my son. He has told me enough."

"I had hoped to stay with you until July, Bob," said Larch when all the boxes were inside, "but my mother is not well. I must return to Topley Landing with Dad and Red Fern. I'll bring in your supplies in October, and I'll try to get up before that if I can get away from the mill for a few days during the summer. There seems to be plenty of trouble in the lake country right now, according to Dad. I'll tell you about it when I see you again."

When I came to pay Red Fern for the supplies, we discovered that I had not found sufficient gold for more than half the food bill, not to mention other necessities.

"Forget it," Larch said. "The fur business was better than usual this winter. Then there was the otter. Maybe you'll strike it rich this summer."

"Thanks. I promise to pan harder after I teach the bears to forage by themselves." Nobody was fooled about the fact that I had been delinquent because of the amount of time I had spent with the bears.

I felt helplessly lonely for a while, knowing that Larch was not across the lake. He was a sensitive son of the wilderness, unusually intelligent, and experienced beyond his years—a true friend and a companion without peer. If the region should become a game preserve, however, he would have to seek winter employment elsewhere. Distasteful as trapping was to him, he often confided to me that he was happiest here because he felt more at ease with both the people and the animals of the inner bush.

It rained for days on end during May. Unlike unseasonal storms, though, which could be frustrating and downright annoying, the constant drip, drip, drip of the rainy season was expected. Day or night, I learned to live with it because it was there when it was supposed to be—warm and life-giving, ancillary to a plentiful range, counterbalance against drought and forest fires. We never let the rain deter our forage hikes as we did just prior to hibernation. I'll admit to seeking shelter during heavy downpours, but the bears dug marsh roots or grazed unperturbed on tender aster and yarrow shoots in the meadows and moors. They were as cheerful and playful as when they were cubs.

As the snowlines retreated with the rains, dwarf dogwood poured forth cascades of white clusters, and the air was scented day and night with mountain rhododendron. Big spherical pasqueflowers broke into blossom the day the larks returned to the upland meadows, while pink calypso orchids and beds of glossy wintergreen were in full flower by the time the population of small hibernators reappeared in the aisles among the trees. Shooting stars, white saxifrage, and fireweed swayed from every fissure along the windy ridges above timberline where the mountain goats had returned to nurse their kids. It was good once more to hear the shrill "wheet-whew" of alpine marmots who had hibernated beneath the high rock moorlands since September; and every pica, who clung to his austere margin of starvation and never did hibernate —even at fifty degrees below zero—seemed to hurl back "Piker!" every time the marmot whistled. Spring had come with a sudden boisterousness of tumult, form, and color.

Persuading myself it was much too early to wade around in water barely above freezing to dig out the meagerest suggestion of gold flakes, I followed the yearlings over a new route of their choosing three times the length and breadth of their forage range of the autumn before. When the full seizure of their hunger struck, their appetites were formidable. They became very serious at the business of working an area of mice, voles, lemmings, fern shoots, bitterroot, arrowroot, birds' eggs, chipmunks, and insects. The trio appropriated and ate any carrion—the remains of prey left by other predators—they discovered, challenging the ownership rights of all other animals. Despite their ravenous hunger, they were extravagantly careless and generally left behind—fortunately for others who had to eat—greater quantities of food than they consumed. A flock of gargling ravens soon learned to follow the affluent bears and thrive on their leavings. We watched a family of otters that lived in a log-jam on a high bank of Hautête Creek about a mile above the beaver dam. Equally wasteful, they would fish diligently, catch a trout, bite off the head, gouge out the liver, and then discard the meaty body of the fish. The habit was especially providential for raccoons, minks, bears wolverines, fishers, and eagles who followed the daily wake of the wastrels. We discovered that the otters indulged in breakfast bright and early, so in order to ply our trade of scavenging to best advantage, we got into the habit of being there before our worthy competitors.

By the middle of June the bears weighed about 150 pounds each. Their chief forage consisted of grass, roots, bracken, and herbs, with enormous hors d'oeuvres of fish and carrion. On every possible occasion Rusty led Dusty and Scratch—with my permission, I must hang my wicked head and confess—into pitched battles with wolves, coyotes, cougars, and single black bears over a carcass of deer, sheep, goat, or wapiti fawn. I fear I may have encouraged them to subscribe to the old adage: "Take from no one what he gives up easily." As a team they were now prepared to back up their hunger with clawed uppercuts and fangs equal to those of any competitor short of the off-limits grizzly. Once the fight was won—in the true tradition of northern violence—the three bears would sit down to the cooperative feast without so much as a snarl at one another. When I approached, their attitude was to move over in order to make room for me at the "table," especially if they had chosen to drag a carcass a mile or more home.

In Rusty I could observe the greatest daily change. During our hikes he would stop and wait for me to catch up, licking my hand or nose when I patted him on the head, ran my fingers through his ruff, or put my arm around his bulky neck. While Dusty and Scratch lay on the sunny southern side of the cabin sleeping in the sun, Rusty would follow me about and proctor whatever activity I was engaged in. Mumbling his satisfaction with everything I did, he was never far from my side. By the fireplace at night he lay against my feet while I read or entered notes into my diary. When I retired we had a running argument because he hadn't yet outgrown the cubhood idea that we could still inhabit the same sleeping bag.

Eventually I lost the struggle, tore out the single bed, and built a mammoth, king-size frame over which I spread blankets and sleeping bag, knowing full well that the moment I yielded to Rusty, the other two would root their way in. I was never more at ease than when sleeping with the bears. They were entirely without odor, without bad breath even two hours after eating overripe carrion, and without any kind of vermin other than ticks which I removed every day anyway. Aside from a little rambunctious eagerness to play when we first went to bed, their nighttime manners were impeccable. Once they began to snore softly, they rarely moved until morning, at which time I received a regular nose nudging when it came time to crawl out for a visit to the otter coign. I cannot recall their ever having deliberately awakened me. My first waking sight each morning was three pairs of shiny, brownish-yellow eyes staring silently and affectionately into my face. Instead of wagging a short tail as a dog would do, each bear engaged in a rapid tapping of the claws of both front feet. Rusty introduced the routine, and the other two took it up at once.

Even during their first moult in late June when their fur shed in great gobs, they seemed to get all their scratching done before we went to bed. I drove two dozen eight-penny nails through a small piece of soft pine and made a currycomb to which I subjected my unobjecting friends twice a day for the moult period. At best they were a ragged, tattered-looking trio before their new fur grew in. In addition to the six-week moult, they were at a particularly gangling age of awkward bowleggedness and clumsiness, with a talent for tripping over their own shadows as they shifted from cub lope to adult shuffle. Had the Humane Society seen them during that period, I'm sure I would have been accused of animal neglect.

As I look back over our life together, I feel certain that that month of June was the happiest time we ever knew. The environment of Canadian springtime at its peak appeared as if it might be unable to withstand the intensity of new life evident in every physical feature of air, water, and earth. Mosquitoes, gnats, deerflies, and no-see-ums were at an all-time minimum because of the severe winter, yet the rest of the world of young animals seemed overpopulated. Each day a flock of mountain goats, led by a venerable old granny instead of some sultan buck, passed along the

beach, then headed up Hautête Creek with a dozen
bouncing kids. Elk, also led by does, began to urge
their fawns toward the upland meadows where the
scrub willows were sprouting juicy, tender buds.
Wolves with wobbly cubs, vixen foxes and their kits,
coyotes with playful whelps, and cow moose with
knock-kneed calves passed the cabin every day on
their way to hunting and pasture ranges along windy
shelves and cobble-fan moraines which were shaped
into alpine meadows in the days when the great
Pleistocene glaciers were spending all their ice.

Long wedges of snow geese, northing to the fringes
of the Arctic, wheeled in to rest a night with the
Canada geese who summered on the sandy jetty at
the mouth of Hautête Creek. Bachelor grouse and
ptarmigan drummed with their wings to attract hens
to the pine brakes above Takla Lake. Cackly, flashing
flights of vagrant magpies and whisky-jacks continually
interrupted the regal silence. The hammering calls of
bitterns invariably preceded the rolling surge of
avalanches, as if the birds might have known what
was about to happen on the gale-torn crags in the
Ominecas. Common in the twilight were adult great
horned owls, most savage of all North American birds
of prey, as they collected hares, birds, bats, and even
small hawks. Owls apparently suffered from compelling
hunger. They were always eating or looking for
something to eat. Many birds, such as sparrows, rails,
snipes, and plovers, were notoriously clumsy fliers;
but not so the great horned owl. He could maneuver
his six-foot wing-spread with amazing speed and skill
through the most complicated forest course. Ptarmigans, moulting out their white winter feathers,
preferred a slow, goose-stepping, pedestrian pace to
flight in all but the direst emergencies. I've always
rather pitied ptarmigans, with their feathered toes:
even in summer they have to roost with their snowshoes
on.

It was a wonderfully balanced, full, lively spring.

As the natural leader of the triplets, Rusty was as
devoted to the responsibilities of leadership as a sheep

dog to his master's flock. In conflicts with other
animals over carrion, he always threw his weight first
with Scratch because he realized his brother was the
weakest of the three. If a ram was about to overtake
Dusty as it evicted her from a sweet vernal meadow,
Rusty would lead Scratch into counterattack. The only
abdication of responsibility I ever observed in the bear
was during attacks by grouse, bitterns, jays, and
whisky-jacks. Under such daily sneak tactics by the
birds, it was every bear for himself—*sauve qui peut*.

It was during that yearling spring, when Rusty began
to shadow my heels, that we developed our closest
rapport and mutual affection. As Dusty and Scratch
looked to Rusty for leadership and defense, so Rusty
looked to me for companionship and approval. At
first I chased him away, because the tendency fell at
odds with my program of weaning the bears toward
independence; but through human weakness on my
part and the persistent, disarming efforts on the part
of the bear to establish the companionship we both
craved, I succumbed to a relationship of inter-
dependence; that would never have happened had
Larch A-Tas-Ka-Nay stayed on at the lake. By the
first of July, nothing of the cub remained in Rusty.
Although it would take three more years for him to
reach bear maturity, he became a serious, tireless friend
that second year of his life, almost an adult. His
greatest joy seemed to express itself in physical
proximity to me.

The yearlings were on their way one morning to
a post-hibernation mud bath near the blueberry and
bearberry barrens above the bog near the creek where
I panned gold, when we heard the most distressing
moans. Approaching what I had always considered
dangerously quick ooze, we found a young cow moose
hopelessly imbedded in the mire. Head and shoulders
above the doughy slime, she appeared exhausted
beyond further struggle. Rusty and I ran back to the
cabin for a rope. From the look in her eyes, she had
plainly given up and was resigned to imminent
suffocation. Lassoing her head and tying the other
end of the rope around a tree, I cut a stout willow

pole to twist as a windlass between the moose and the tree. When the slipknot cut deeply enough into her throat to cut off her wind, she struggled. As she kicked, groaned, rolled, and splashed, I took up on the slack until at last she got one foot on solid sod. With hope thus restored, the muddy black empress pulled herself out, reversed her ears, snorted, and charged me, not for having saved her life, but as the nearest living thing upon which to vent her anger at the mire. Nothing parallels the rage of a humiliated moose. I had already treed the bears and planned my own defensive strategy against what I guessed would be a volcanic disposition once she was free. As I flagged the moose to chase me around and around the tree, her neck rope became shorter and shorter. Unable to reason that she could turn the other way and wipe me out, she literally reached the end of her rope, slamming helplessly into the trunk and falling with such a deadly thud that I feared she might have broken her neck. At that instant all her rage turned into fright; thus when I reached around the tree and cut the rope, she jumped to her feet and loped away with a short necklace of Manila hemp.

June was a wonderful month for collecting mushrooms and for digging and drying wild onions, chicory, and dandelion root. For the bears there were more grass shoots and fern fiddlenecks than they wanted to eat. They peeled an endless supply of sweet-willow bark and lay on their bellies sucking nectar from lupine flowers. They licked up resin drippings beneath every spruce and hemlock for an odd variation in diet which nature apparently required. I boiled the roots of Solomon's seal and cattail with sorrel and watercress for myself as well as the bears. They lapped up the mushy puree with great gusto but raced out immediately after each such feast and sought green haws and the hills of vinegar ants. I supposed it was a natural craving to neutralize all that starch.

Like the otters, a pair of neighboring ospreys were either extravagantly improvident or insufferably fussy when it came to fishing. By actual count, they took between sixteen and twenty-four large trout per day, taloning the fish up to their eyrie, tearing them apart, and feeding them to their young. The amount of "crumbs" which fell over the side of the osprey "table" composed a considerable part of each day's calorie count for Rusty, Dusty, and Scratch. No amount of ursine gluttony, however, overcame the discretion that warned them *not* to climb that particular tree. The ospreys had communicated.

Indians, prospectors, and old-time nesters in the back country had all spoken at one time or another of "bear trees." I often watched the unintelligible antics of bears around specific trees in widely separated reaches of the woods. Legend had it that such trees were woodland bulletin boards where bruin could catch up on local bear gossip, but the yearlings as well as other bears yielded evidence that the "bear tree," usually a jack pine, sugar pine, sugar maple, or other species that exuded sweet, aromatic sap when clawed, was nothing more than a "sweets bar" upon which each greedy bear was attempting to stake a private claim. That the bear tree might have some communicative function, however, was demonstrated one morning when I observed two adult boars at the foot of one of the trees. The larger of the two stood erect, put his forearms around the tree, sniffed, licked, and chewed for a minute or two, then left. The second bear awaited his turn—only because he was smaller— then repeated the performance of the first. The yearlings followed suit in the order of pecking rights: Rusy, Dusty, and Scratch.

Obviously a bear embracing, chewing, or clawing the tree would leave some of his scent and hair thereabouts which would be of great interest to subsequent callers. The yearlings always urinated several times near such trees. Strangely enough, in a stand of any given species, only one tree would be selected by all black bears in the vicinity as the "bear tree." On our range one such jack pine had been girdled and killed many years before our arrival by the gnawing-clawing activity, yet the barkless trunk continued to rally the bear population to the monument.

After all, cats commit silly gyrations over catnip,

dogs kick up a fuss over dogbane, and people do the strangest things under the influence of *several* plants!

Late one afternoon in June I was busy doodling plans for a new smoke shed when I heard the yearlings whining and gurgling near the porch. This always meant they were excitedly pleased about something. By habit I went to investigate.

When I stepped to the porch, I received one of the happiest surprises I've ever known. In a noisy, awkwardly strutting round of excitement pranced three yearling bears, while around my head and shoulders flew three yearling robins.

Since the bears had played around the robins so often since the days of the old cardboard carton, it was perhaps not so remarkable that they recognized the birds and obviously rejoiced at the sight of their return. Birds must release distinctive, identifying odors as other animals do. Otherwise I don't know how the yearlings could have recognized the three robins as the ones I had plucked from the forest fire and subsequently raised. Robins had crossed our yard for a week without arousing the slightest interest, yet suddenly three individual birds recalled specific experience.

Contemplating the episode for many days thereafter, I marveled more at the mysterious powers of memory and navigating ability that had guided the birds in returning across thousands of miles, as some pets will, to the hand that raised them.

10

The Bountiful Range

Our robins were fully grown, two cocks and a speckled
hen. From the shelf behind the cabin that had held
them when they were fledglings, they wooed wilderness
mates. Even during nesting, our three friends returned
daily for afternoon sunbaths on the shelf where I kept
a pan of cereal. When their own offspring left their
nests, they too claimed space on the provident, sunny
retreat. Many the morning wide-eyed window-tappers
made a predawn announcement that the pan was empty. It was unthinkable to turn them down.

The only serious fight that ever occurred between
the yearlings happened the time Dusty tried to horn
in on a clutch of grouse eggs Scratch had found in
the brodiaeas and lupines at the edge of the upper
meadow. While the two were mauling and chewing
one another, Rusty ate the dozen eggs—shell and all—
before I could intervene. After the five-minute bran-
nigan, the two shook themselves, licked each other's
wounds, and looked about as if to say, "Now, let's
see; just what were we fighting about?" Rusty and
I sat in the middle of the meadow waiting to proceed
with the morning walk.

Nest robbing continued, however, to present a bone
of considerable contention. To put across the concept
that all birds and their nests were to be left strictly
alone, I led the yearlings to specific nests and made
it clear they were off limits. They never robbed a nest
that I had specifically declared taboo, but they found
others I didn't know about. They had been so easy
to teach in some areas. Consider, for example, the

robins. To prove they were capable of educated attitudes and responses, the bears ignored all robins. Yet they chased other species except those that had pecked them when they were cubs. Why they refused to give up nest robbing, knowing my consistent reaction to the deplorable practice, is a question I still can't answer.

It was during this yearling summer that the bears established themselves in one way or another with neighboring creatures. If they were hungry, as a trio they muscled food away from wolves, coyotes, lions, and other black bears—except dams with cubs. They sniffed out carrion that our distant grizzly neighbor had buried, but they would surrender whatever they were eating if the venerable old rogue with the flinty personality happened to show up in the flesh. It must have been fun to steal from the patient silver tip, because no other woodland creature had the guts it took to violate his domain. The yearlings did swim and bathe with him occasionally when he came down to the lake, so no real enmity existed between the two species. Dusty had genuine faith in most of her animal neighbors and would crawl on her belly to show her friendly attitude toward foxes, martens, and raccoons, who always frustrated her overtures by distrusting her. Rusty never traded upon his ability to terrorize his fellow creatures. For a yearling black bear, he was too serious—almost as if he had been charged with some vast responsibility. Instead of yielding to a yearling's compulsion to roll every rollable object, he would assume sentry duty or sit next to me while the other two engaged in the sport. Scratch, on the other hand, was the accomplished buffoon who threw his weight around every time he could find a sucker to bluff; but when a neighboring lynx, coyote, or wolverine called his hand, he would sometimes climb sixty feet up the nearest conifer, coughing, snarling, and showing his teeth.

We were sitting in the blueberry barren one morning when another hefty yearling approached. Since there was no castanet champing of teeth, which was Rusty's usual way of expressing wrath, I decided to sit by and observe developments. Although the newcomer nudged, rolled, whined, and gurgled, Rusty, Dusty, and Scratch refused to acknowledge his pretentious display. Bored by the rustic's comedy, they yawned like teen-agers in church. Finally Rusty got up, pointed with his nose—the signal for the rest of us to follow—and led the way back to the cabin without finishing the day's foraging. The other bear followed near my heels to within a hundred yards of our hill, at which time Rusty stopped, turned around, and gave the trespasser a single significant look. The stranger not only took the hint, but was still kicking up pebbles at full gallop the last time I looked back.

The bears were expert in starting things they could not or would not finish, and often relieved their boredom with nose-poking occupations that were likely to produce unpredictable surprises. They never seemed to learn that results with a porcupine were always the same, no matter what strategy one might adopt in the hope of getting revenge for previous engagements. The only members of our neighborhood who ever convinced the bears of their total and irrevocable defeat were the skunks. And try as they always did, the bears couldn't sneak up on the wary old hermit bighorn who inhabited the rocky cliffs behind the upland meadows. The sheep was an unworthy adversary with no sense of humor when it came to bears as a race.

Then there was the three-toed arctic woodpecker who drummed for hours on end up and down the old dead tree across Hautête Creek. The bears despised the monotonous tapping. Only the devil himself could have inspired them to swim the creek time after time, forgetting that they would be unable to climb the slick, barkless trunk when wet. Thus they were never able to finish the project of chasing the woodpecker away.

Contrary to most bears, the trio enjoyed all forms of stroking, petting, rubbing, and holding. One way I showed affection was to grasp a bear around the muzzle and to shake as two men would shake hands. The only trouble with the greeting was that they also demanded every other form of patting and fondling which they thought should accompany the gesture. It was no longer physically possible for me to wrestle, spar, or engage in other roughhousing with them, since they had grown out of my league. I could take no chances of an accident with no possibility of any aid reaching me before late summer.

I kept the cabin door closed by means of a wooden bar which slid along through a slender trough and entered a casement slot near the weather jam. A short, round dowel ran through the bar as well as the door for interior or exterior opening and shutting. One day I decided it would save me an enormous amount of ups and downs to teach the bears to open and close the door when they wanted to pass in or out. In the presence of Dusty and Scratch, I showed Rusty how to open the lock from the inside as well as the outside. He learned almost instantly to slide the bar backward or forward by taking the dowel between his teeth. The other two were quick to imitate him. Ever afterward they were able to let themselves in or out whenever they wished; but try as I did, I was never able to teach one of those bears to *close* the door—let alone lock it—once it had been opened.

July came and went, but Larch A-Tas-Ka-Nay had evidently not been able to get away from his work. Fortunately I worked out a way to divert a part of Hautête Creek into a new channel so I could dig down to bedrock and run greater quantities of mud and gravel over the sluice baffles. In thirty days I recovered enough gold to pay for supplies for two years. That was what Larch's father had suggested in the first place, but I had thought the task too great for one man until I actually tried it.

On August first an airplane circled the cabin, dropped to the lake on pontoons, and taxied up to the beach. It was Dan Yeager, an independent bush pilot whom I had met two years before when I was prospecting tributaries of the Liard in the Northwest Territories.

"Heard you were in here living with a herd o' bears, Bob," he said as we secured the plane's wings against any sudden blast of wind.

"That means you've been in Topley Landing. What brings you down here, Dan?"

"Survey boys. Big argument in Parliament over this region being made into a provincial park or game refuge."

"Great guns! I hope they don't back out on us now!"

"So do I, but opposition's growing by the day. They say a park in here would be used by very few people. But the way it is, hunters, trappers, miners, and timbermen make good use of the land."

"And supposedly intelligent politicians buy that hogwash."

"They believe what the fattest lobby tells them to believe, not what's best for the country in the long run."

Suddenly the bears joined us on the beach. With hackles standing on end from ruff to rump, they walked slowly and with stiff legs around Dan, sniffed every inch of him they could reach on all fours, then to his terror they stood up and explored his cap, the back of his neck, and his shoulders. Satisfied at last that he might be classified in the category of friend, they shuffled over to explore the airplane.

"I know how to make friends with bears," he said as he reached into the cockpit and withdrew a sack of hard candy. My heart sank within me, but too late. This innocent gesture was exactly what I didn't want. A bear never forgets a betrayal of friendship, never forgets a handout of sweets. They would thereafter approach anyone, believing the goodie to be the reward. Well and good until they waddled up to a monster seeking a bear rug.

I had the feeling Dan had flown in to tell me something he hadn't yet hinted, so I insisted he come up to the cabin and spend the night. The bears were close on his heels, but they knew enough to sit down and behave like a lady and gentlemen once we entered the door.

"How are things at Topley Landing?" I asked over coffee and bannock cakes.

"That's what I really wanted to see you about, Bob.

Larch A-Tas-Ka-Nay is in trouble. He took a passionate stand in favor of the park. The lumber company fired him. The packers and trappers are trying to run him out of the country. The mining outfits have blacklisted him. He's in Victoria most of the time trying to contact members of Parliament to solicit their votes when they reconvene. Took every dime his father and some Indian named Red Fern could scrape up to send him down there. The mill tied the can on Red Fern too when they found out he was helping Larch. Local Chilcotins and Beavers are split. Madder than hornets at one another. Some say they'd make more from cheechakos if there was a park. Others want to keep on trapping, hunting, or working for the mill."

"Dan, I've panned out about a thousand dollars in placer. Can you get it to Red Fern on your way out?"

"I sure can, but Larch and his friends are gonna need more than that is they're to win. They don't know yet where the Hudson's Bay Company will throw their weight. Now here's what old man A-Tas-Ka-Nay has up his sleeve. Says there's a lot o' gold in the Hautête. He'd like to bring in a dozen Indians during August and sluice it for all it's worth, but won't do it unless you agree. Says you could use Larch's cabin on the other side o' the lake till the first o' September. That would give the Indians enough money for the winter and send several more to Victoria for a show o' strength. If that's agreeable with you, I'll start crow-hoppin' 'em in tomorrow."

I brought out the coffee can full of gold, helped him relaunch his plane, and told him I'd be on the other side of the lake by noon the following day.

Red Fern and the elder A-Tas-Ka-Nay arrived by bateau the next afternoon. Dan Yeager flew the twelve other Indians over in three trips, then flew in food and equipment during the following two days. It did not seem that the pilot ever slept.

Larch had told me during the winter about a creek less than a mile down the lake from his cabin where he had seen "color." As soon as I could break the bears in on a new range, I began to dig and pan every possible daylight hour. The pickings were slim indeed. The yearlings acted as if they understood that some kind of crisis existed. Never once during that month did they leave my side. Red Fern and Peter came over once a week to report on the project and to see if everything was all right with me and the yearlings.

One afternoon in late August—I was never quite sure about dates up there even though I kept a fairly accurate diary—a large twin-engine airplane landed on the lake, taxied up to Larch's beach, and tied up. It was a government plane. When the bears and I strode up from the "diggin's," there stood Larch, two Parliament deputies, three officials from the Bureau of Lands and Forests, and two high-ranking officers of the Royal Canadian Mounted Police. When the bears recognized Larch, they all but tore his clothes off. Within a few minutes Red Fern and Peter arrived in their bateau. As we handed Larch our gold, I explained to the officials that we were digging almost night and day to keep our friend in Victoria where he could work on the worthy cause. They were not well impressed by my life with the bears but agreed that the region should be at least a game reserve, preferably a provincial park because of its scenic attractions and wildlife.

"I believe you have made your point, Mr. A-Tas-Ka-Nay," announced the man who seemed to be leading the group. "Shall we be on our way before these damned bears get hungry?"

I was proud of Rusty, Dusty, and Scratch, who had wandered with regal dignity and superb manners through the crowd as many a hand delivered friendly pats and strokes. There was not a bristle raised, not a snarl issued—only the most mournful of cries when Larch boarded the plane.

"Take care, Bob, and carry on," he said as we shook hands. "I'll be back as soon as the fight is won. You've no idea how many people have to be sold."

Two days later Red Fern began hauling the Indians out by bateau. I learned much later that Dan Yeager's plane had fallen into the Liard River near Fort Simpson after a faulty take-off. Dan's body was never recovered.

"Left our extras in your cache, Bob," Red Fern said on his last trip out. "We'll be back in October with your winter supplies—paid for in advance this time. The operation was a great success, but we cleaned out your diggin's."

"What about your jobs?" I asked.

"I'll be with the Indian Agency in Vanderhoof, but I don't know what these other men and their families will do. That's our next problem."

It required two trips by canoe to get my things back to our own side of the lake, because the bears begged so fervently to accompany me both times. That meant approximately seven hundred pounds of bear, in addition to my own weight and gear, paddled fifteen miles. Red Fern had offered to get us back, but I declined because I knew he had more important things to do at the end of a long journey. What a ludicrous picture we must have made! Holding the gunwales with their front paws, three large yearlings sat one behind the other along the bottom of the canoe. One medium-sized man sat on the stern wedge, paddling his heart out barely to move across the smooth surface.

By the first of September it was physically impossible for me to follow the bears on their daily forage, because the advancing season made it necessary for them to extend their range. One morning, at the end of about four miles, the bears stopped and seemed to hold a short conference. Rusty came back to where I sat puffing for breath on a log. What Larch had predicted about the hourglass, I had to face. Rusty climbed up alongside me. The yearlings had demonstrated to my satisfaction that I was by then little more than an ornament as far as their protection was concerned, so I sent them on their way for the first time without me, trusting that Rusty would assume full charge. I began to know how the osprey and the great horned owl and the eagle must have felt when they gave their sons and daughters that first shove from the nest.

Every possible gruesome calamity passed through my imagination before the bears returned to the cabin at sundown. They were visibly fatigued, but round-gutted with carrion. From dried froth along their muzzles, I assumed there had been some wholesomely subversive activities. Disregarding their weariness, the three yanked me from the porch and bowled me over into the dry fescue in front of the cabin. They nibbled, licked, and pawed me as if they had been gone a week. When I yelled the stop signal "No!" at having my beard pulled, they raced one another around the hill, climbed the tallest hemlock, slid back to the ground, then lumbered over to where I was still sitting in the hay. With face-wide grins, they fell into a heaving mound of groaning meat and fur.

It was generally Scratch's lot to end up on the bottom of any hog pile, which was no inconvenience when they were fifty-pound cubs; but toward the end of their yearling summer, Rusty and Dusty had grown too heavy to pile up on him at the same time. Hissing and spitting, Scratch would vomit a part of what he had eaten when they felt he had earned a waylaying.

Toward late afternoon on the second day of the yearlings' unrestricted roaming, I walked down the beach in hopes of meeting them. When I reached the berry barrens, I decided to strike uphill to the first meadow so as to circle back to the cabin by way of the game trail—a habitual route over which I assumed they would return home. I was about to enter the forest above the meadow when peculiar yelps and growls caused me to continue to a willow thicket at the upper end of the moor. Sneaking in to avoid being seen, I surprised the bears in the act of settling an earlier grudge with a pair of contemptuous badgers. As Scratch moved in for a two-in-one swat, the male badger's powerful jaws clamped like a steel trap around the bear's front paw. During the confusion that followed, Rusty and Dusty took out after the female, who ran into her den under a boulder. Instead of coming to Scratch's rescue, they tried to dig out the escapee. Scratch stood erect, suspending the squirming animal at arm's length, and yelling for help as he turned around and around. At that point I entered the fight and began flogging the badger with my walking stick. Seeing himself once again at a disadvantage, the badger dropped to the ground and fled into the brush. When we returned to the cabin, Scratch brought me his bleeding paw, which we soaked in hot salty water for the evening.

Each morning the bears walked with me to an Ice Age gravel dump two miles down the lake where I was operating a paying dry placer. They waited until I began my work before going through our ritual of saying good-bye for the day. Convinced that they could not inveigle me into accompanying them, and not understanding exactly why, they circled on all fours, stood up, and made sounds not unike the softened bray of a donkey. That simply meant they were hungry. After returning quick hugs, they would slowly depart for distant canyons, meadows, and barrens, stopping often to look back, rather pathetically hoping I might change my mind.

To some, the bowlegged black bear with front feet turned in may look like a fool and act like a buffoon, but none of his farcical exhibitions are intrinsically out of keeping with his character. He is indeed the most peaceful neighbor in the forest and belies the frazzled cliché, "as cross as an old bear." The heaviest animal on his feet in the North American forest, the bear walks flatfooted on the entire soft, naked soles of his paws, and that is why he can sneak over an acre of dry twigs and leaves and sit down beside you without your knowing he is there. The bear knows how to put all his living into today, and his temperament often includes a reckless sense of humor unparalleled outside man himself. A bear is intentionally funny and appears to enjoy a good practical joke, yet a point of great significance in this respect is that bears, like dogs and monkeys, do not enjoy bearing the brunt of a prank that is not initiated by another bear. In fact, otherwise harmless bears have been known to punish pranksters.

Except when eating carrion, the yearlings were among the cleanest wild animals I have known. They wallowed primarily for good contact with the earth. It helped dislodge any fleas, ticks, or lice they might have picked up from other associates. In the bath that always followed wet or dry wallowing, any remaining parasites were drowned. During all but the coldest months they went into the lake or Hautête Creek at least once a day; and instead of rolling in dirt or weeds when they emerged from the water, they climbed a tree and stretched out on a limb where the wind dried their thick fur clean and fluffy.

There is a species of *white* black bear in western British Columbia, known as Kermode's bear, who is so clean by habit that he spends a part of each day cleaning his native white toenails!

A great many people have asked how I engendered obedience in these freeborn animals, especially after the first year. I should like to state categorically that I never demanded any obedience as such. What I sought was an endless flow of cooperation through their understanding exactly what I wanted from them. Their good manners inside the cabin was merely a matter of early training and the thought of violating the rules never crossed their minds, once they understood that I would not tolerate the slightest infraction. They were reliable both to me and to one another because they knew from early cubhood that I expected the exercise of that native characteristic. Reliability became a habit. It took Rusty, a wilderness-born black bear, to teach me that rational communication of certain concepts does not necessarily require words or symbols.

They were not always brave. They harbored phobias and passed through periods of hallucinations that were almost funny, except that I never laughed at them once I learned they were sensitive about them. When the whisky-jacks discovered that the bears would flee in terror when the flock concentrated upon power-diving and pecking plump rear ends, the birds took sinister pleasure in driving the trio either into the cabin or deep into the woods; whereupon I quit feeding the whisky-jacks.

As a young man, I used to hike through the desert hills of Sonora and Baja California; and because of snakes, I always walked with an alpenstock. The habit being such a pleasant one, I continued it through the Rockies and on up into British Columbia and Alberta. For some reason I have been unable to assess, the cubs took a poignant dislike to the walking stick. At times they became skittish, took to a tree, and refused to come down for an hour when I took the stick on our early hikes. When I tried to point out the harmless qualities of the willow cane, they bit it and cuffed it. The trio always gave the cane a wide berth as it leaned against the log ends at one corner of the cabin, an attitude generally held by animals who have been clobbered. I once had a dog that would pick up my cane in his mouth and bring it to me when he wanted me to take him for a walk, but not the bears. For no reason known to me, they deplored its existence.

Thunder also alarmed them, but with some reason. We had witnessed two major lightning strikes near the cabin that second summer. The yearlings were showered with bark which the violent element had ripped from the trunk of a fir. Although they suffered no pain, they cringed and bawled and ever afterward sought a dark corner inside the cabin during thunderstorms. Lightning ashes made them shriek, but while new charges accrued, curiosity brought out three wooly heads to wonder where the next flash would occur.

Whenever we robbed a bee tree—which was every time we could locate one—I watched all three bears devour thousands of bees; in fact, I often feared the hives might be decimated to the point of destruction. Yet I observed girlish panic in all three bears at the approach of a single bee in an open meadow. As cubs, they hadn't learned to erect their fur or to cover their noses and naked soles with honey to avoid being stung on those vulnerable parts. They gleaned each fragment of wilderness knowledge the hard way.

Early in October Larch arrived with my winter supplies. The bears knew him the moment he set foot upon the beach, and the welcome they accorded him was in the form of a compound roughing-up in the grand style of bears. A stranger would have thought he was being attacked and killed on the sand beneath the pile of roaring throats and mauling arms.

Larch looked tired, serious, and lean.

"How is your family, Larch?" I asked as we headed for the cabin.

"Mother died. That was why I returned to Topley Landing from Victoria. Dad doesn't look as if he'll be able to take the winter. The Chilkotins have demanded that I take him and myself to other parts unless we both want to be killed."

"And what about the park?"

"Looks good for a game reserve, any day now, but I doubt if Parliament will risk an appropriation this season for park status. Politicians are all alike. They want the issue to cool off during the summer when they are not in session. Sometimes they keep it in deep freeze for the winter when they meet. So they'll try it first as a refuge. They've mosied around up here and felt certain pulses. They know what side their bread's buttered on. I don't think we have anything to worry about."

"What will you do, Larch?"

In the dark brown depths of his saddened eyes, I sensed hidden undertones which at the time I could not possibly have understood.

11

Dusty's Boyfriend

Larch was no longer the happy, carefree woodsman
of the year before. When he spoke of the opposing
lumber industry he said, "Sawmill people speak in
pained tones of overmature timber that must be
salvaged. There's no such thing as overmature timber
except in the lopsided language of commerce."

When he spoke about the Indian community of
Topley Landing, it was with bitterness and disappointment. He knew that if the Indians had been of
one accord, the issue of the park would not have
alienated the mill people and mining interests to such
an extent that they brought in replacements for those
who were discharged—not even Beaver replacements,
but Kitamats from Prince Rupert and Kwakiutls from
Bella Coola who spoke Salish and attended secret
society rites. Potlatch festivals were in progress; but
the Sekanis, Sarsis, Chilkotins, and Babines—all
Beavers—had been warned not to attend. The Tahltans
and Kaskas were still undecided with which faction
to smoke the calumet.

At my insistence Larch finally answered my question
concerning his future.

"I have applied to the Bureau of Lands and Forests
to join the Forest Patrol. I'm nearly out of money."

During the week Larch stayed with us, we trans-
ferred most of his personal belongings from his cabin
to mine since he would not be spending the winter
at Takla Lake. On one return crossing back to Hautête
Creek, he precipitately hurled every piece of his trapping equipment into the deepest part of the lake. We

were about to launch for another trip when Rusty and Scratch begged to go along. Dusty accompanied us to Larch's boat but refused to board. As we pulled away from the shore, she turned and disappeared into the forest behind the cabin.

"I've been watching Dusty," Larch said when we were about halfway across. "She has a boyfriend who meets her up on the game trail."

"Snow foam!" I retorted. "Black bears aren't fully mature until they are four years old and females never mate until they are at least three."

"Aha!" he exclaimed. "What you don't know is that female yearlings begin to court eligible bachelors sometimes a year or so in advance of actual mating. Don't be surprised when little Dusty elopes! The stick is like the tree that bore it."

"I'll dread the day she leaves," I said, "yet that's exactly what I've hoped for all of them. I've expected them to identify less with me now that they forage greater distances alone. The urge to seek a mate will break up our little family."

"She may bring him home with her one day. There are such things as bear colonies, you know."

The day was warm yet crisp in an October sort of way, so we hiked with Rusty and Scratch up to a spur of the Hogem Range on the Pacific Divide for distant views of Purvis and Tchentlo lakes. Aspens, sumacs, cottonwoods, dogwoods, beeches, and maples had been bitten by the first frosts and were then in their gayest autumn wardrobes. On the final ridge the yearlings exhumed a bighorn ewe, apparently a grizzly bear cache not yet "ripe" enough to satisfy the more seasoned bon vivant.

"I hope his nibs doesn't show up while these two clean the choicest cuts," Larch said with a smile.

The words were barely out of his mouth—I hadn't even had time to comment that the simplest formula for incurring a grizzly's hatred was to swipe his cache—when a great silver-tip boar rushed to within twenty feet of Rusty and Scratch. The dignity of the somber giant's fearless bearing was truly regal as he reared and towered a full seven feet to survey his domain invaded and disputed by these two cheechakos. Puffing like a blast furnace, the old monarch suddenly made the most of the capabilities of his lungs and voice. The two yearlings had met grizzlies before and knew the hob Old Buster could raise with one accurate clout; thus they considered it no dilution of masculinity to barge down the canyon and climb a tree while his roar still shook the forest.

Contrary to popular notions in some circles, the grizzly could have climbed the tree and knocked them out of it had he wanted to, but all he did was grumble at the bole.

Grizzlies turn into a cyclone; only after deliberate provocation, not mere inconvenience. Like that of all bears, their temper is defensive rather than aggressive. Pound for pound, they are the fiercest North American mammals in combat, even more so than the larger Alaskan Kodiak or big brown bear, which is their closest natural relative. Weighing between six hundred and one thousand pounds, a grizzly can drag with ease a quarter-ton elk carcass. Only the most rigid protection can now save this magnificent animal from extinction. On the treeless barrens of his habitat, he makes all too conspicuous a target for the long-range, high-power rifle with telescopic sights.

Larch and I hid while the grizzly returned from the eviction of Rusty and Scratch and reburied the sheep. Otherwise the bear might have thought we too were implicated in the sacking of his future meal. Still mumbling to himself and casting one last glance toward the treed yearlings, the hard-boiled old grizzly, inflexible, suspicious, yet petulantly timid, shuffled off to his rocky ledge where he could sit on a glacier-carved throne and survey every approach to his realm from both sides of the Divide. No natural allies could force him to abdicate his authority.

When we arrived at my cabin just after sundown, Dusty was sitting on her haunches by the door. Her shy boyfriend was nowhere in sight. She led off immediately toward the forage range, looked back, then returned to repeat the maneuver, which was her way of telling us she was hungry and wanted us to accompany her on a midnight search for food. We conceded her a mile down the beach before turning back. Rusty continued with her, but Scratch ambled back with Larch and me. They seemed to be resuming their unproctored wandering for the two to four weeks remaining in the season, foraging by night and returning before noon the following day. Scratch didn't like the idea, but venturing forth alone during the day was even less appealing. After two days he joined his brother and sister. At first I missed sleeping with the bears, but I knew I should have to get accustomed to it. Happy to stretch out on a bed of dry needles on the sunny afternoon side of the cabin, they seemed to have forgotten about our king-sized bed inside.

At the end of a week, my restless friend Larch packed his boat, delivered an eloquent good-bye, and headed down the windy lake. Overhead thousands of Canada geese trumpeted their ancient tune as they winged into the international flyways for warm Mexican *lagunas*. Most reluctant to leave the north woods were the robins. The summer had been good. They had raised their families with but few losses to gray owls and marsh hawks. A neighbor had lost her entire clutch to a day-feeding weasel. Thanks to prodigious crops of grubs, worms, ants, and beetles, our robins were all fat and in good condition for the long flight. Where three ragged survivors of the forest fire had tottered the year before, fifteen of the world's champion insect killers now stood poised for migration to the sunny, southern foothills of the Sierra Madre del Occidente or the San Pedro Martir.

One noon, when the yearlings returned from their forage, I got my first glimpse of Dusty's boyfriend, who came as far as the edge of the clearing behind the cabin. He was a glossy, dark-cinnamon brown. Apparently Rusty and Scratch had accepted him, since he joined them every day somewhere near the beginning of their walk. He probably dozed in the forest until they were ready to go again. In my mind I referred to him as the phantom, he was so hard to see. The bears did not always return at precisely the same hour so by the time I was aware of their bowlegged trundling down the path, the phantom had already slipped into the anonymity of the understory of shrubbery and vines. Though I scoured every inch of the landscape with binoculars, he was impossible to locate. Hoping for more intimate information, I accompanied the yearlings evening after evening, thinking surely they had some specific rendezvous along their forage route, but the phantom lover failed to appear. Still I had the feeling the new bear joined them every day.

As the mild Indian summer of October advanced with increasingly chilly, windy days and freezing nights, it seemed that the bears wanted to be at my heels more of the time—another of their sprees of unexplained madness. As I fished the big salmon runs up the Hautête and smoked spinner-hooked steelhead, the three nudged me more often for attention than for fish heads and guts. Physically, they were in better shape than they had been at hibernation time the year before. When I sat enjoying the sun on the lee side of the cabin, it was with three huge wooly heads on my lap until my legs went to sleep from the weight. Although they continued to forage at night, they cut it short to be back to the cabin by early morning. They were never out of sight until sundown. Rusty took to returning at dawn to let himself in for a short cuddle while waiting for the sun to thaw out the night's frost.

Those were busy days. The water became too cold to continue the frenzied search for gold, so I devoted most of the daylight hours to sawing deadfalls and quarter-wedging the sawn sections, which had to be carried and stacked under the wood shelter. With little prospect of a moose or an elk that winter due to an almost total migration before the hunting season, I required roughly two hundred pounds of smoked trout and salmon. In any case, although Larch had left a rifle, I wouldn't deliberately shoot a game animal unless he was hopelessly wounded. The berry crop had been too poor to harvest for drying, but Larch had mysteriously anticipated the lack and had stocked my cache with extra dried prunes, figs, peaches, and raisins. His purchases had been far more intelligent than mine from the standpoint of balanced meals and tasty tidbits.

On the morning of the twenty-fifth of October, according to a diary entry, I got my first detailed look at Dusty's boyfriend. He was a prime four-year-old, weighing about four hundred pounds, a little on the stocky side, which I attributed to prehibernation fat; and, like Rusty, he was of a cinnamon strike. Color aberrations common among Canadian black bears included cinnamon, champagne, beige, and dark brown. There were no true blacks. As Dusty and her spooky lover stood in the path not fifty yards behind the cabin, I was impressed by the size of his ears, which looked like baseball catchers' mitts. He moved them constantly as if he had to shift their position in order to hear what might be going on behind him. The two bears engaged in serious head-shaking and grunting for five minutes before they both stood up on their hind legs and placed their front paws on one another's shoulders for perhaps ten seconds. Dusty then loped into the cabin area, and her boyfriend—who by then I called Spooky—disappeared into the underbrush at one side of the trail.

During the next two days, Dusty did everything to prevail upon Spooky to join our circle. One evening after supper I was sitting in the middle of the bed with Rusty and Scratch. After having opened the door, Dusty stood on the porch grumbling at her beau. The wind coming through the door was biting cold. Finally she gave up and joined her brothers and me as if throwing up her hands and declaring, "Oh, to heck with him!" Spooky edged up to the steps, gingerly crossed the porch, and poked an inquisitive nose into an atmosphere that reeked of man. Dusty, Scratch, and I looked on and waited; but Rusty was not about to share the wealth, affection, or shelter with any boyfriend of Dusty's. When he growled at Spooky, the timid bear scampered away into the forest.

After the wind died down the next afternoon, the three yearlings and I went to snooze in the sun on the south side of the cabin. We had been there perhaps a quarter of an hour when Spooky walked out of the woods and circled the clearing at least six times, passing within ten feet of us. Although Rusty and Scratch whined and chattered their teeth as the magnificent creature slowly inched by, Dusty was apparently pretending she neither saw nor heard him. Her only move was a slight dilation of the nostrils when the big bear begged for her attention. The yearlings were expert in the communication of a general mood to one another. At last, as if fired from the barrel of a cannon, snarling and frothing at the mouth, Dusty shot after Spooky, bit and clawed him until he retreated into the darkest part of the forest. She returned at once, lay down next to me, and promptly began to snore. Dusty was simply not of a mind to receive her suitor that day. Although jealous and often possessive, however, the young bear never stored up permanent grudges or enmity toward other bears, regardless of momentary rage.

Many indications pointed to a late but severe winter, if we could believe old-timers' tales of what constituted a "sure sign." According to Larch, all portents of things to come fascinated the Beaver Indians. They ate up anything that had to do with legend or the supernatural but never believed a word of it. Nevertheless, it was easy to entertain the old beliefs when very specific signs were right there in our front and back yards. Alarming indeed was a south-migrating herd of fifty wapiti which passed single file along the lakeshore—all chewing their cuds as they walked. Such an act was peculiar to elk prior to severe winters—according to sourdoughs. Despite sun and moon halos and raveled mare's tails, there had been no rain and no "black" frost in October, a "clear-cut indication" of rough months ahead. Summer cicadas and crickets came out and sang in broad daylight in late October (until the bears located them and ate them), an "infallible" forecast of cataclysm, according to the Tahltan shamans. The picas seemed to be warehousing unusually large harvests, and the squirrels had cut and piled ten-foot stacks of green cones. The marmots and golden-mantled ground squirrels had gone into hibernation by the middle of September. To the sourdough such behavior was oracular. Hadn't all the water birds except the stormy petrels left early? Why had the crustaceous lichens or "rock tripe" flattened out so soon? Why hadn't the bull moose bugled during the big autumn rutting duels? Could there be such a thing as a *silent* rutting season in the north woods except as a premonitor of boreal disaster? Surely at least some of these phenomena could survive debunking.

Strangely though, I've kept written records of these "signs" for many years as a sort of hobby, and not one of them has ever proven to be an accurate herald of unusual weather. Trained meteorologists with whom I have discussed the "signs" agree that plants and animals have no way of predicting the characteristics of any season—hot, cold, wet, dry, short, or long.

The first snow came as a twenty-four-hour fall, but the weather moderated almost immediately, melting the drifts into the dry ground. During the warm days that followed, the bears bounded and rolled with delight when I took them for afternoon strolls along the clean beach or into the silent upland meadows above timberline. Having climbed a long spur perhaps three miles behind the cabin, I sat down between Rusty and Scratch in the lee of a rocky ledge. The bears merely minced around at eating in late October, exerting very little effort to round up a full meal. We watched Dusty walk slowly back down through a monotonous tundra of sphagnum and blueberry to timberline. Spooky suddenly appeared for a brief sparring. When we decided to return, Dusty and her inamorato kept a good quarter of a mile ahead. I had never seen such a timid bear.

Not only was he timid, Spooky was as clement as

a hamster. Although he never allowed me to approach closer than fifty feet, I was able to observe him better than he supposed through binoculars. His all but dainty eating habits, his gentle lick across the bridge of Dusty's nose, his careful placement of a paw on her shoulder, his two-arm shield against her tomboy exuberance were all in such diametric contrast to Dusty's uninhibited, roistering behavior, that at times I felt a strong compassion for him.

Never was my parental coaching more clearly brought home to roost than the day Spooky brought the carcass of a kid goat to the clearing behind the cabin to share with Dusty. When the three yearlings got a whiff of fresh, red meat at the same instant, they pigeon-toed over toward Spooky, who was standing upright holding the kid's scruff between his teeth. As if by signal when the trio had sauntered nonchalantly to within six feet of the older bear, they leaped through the air as a unit and landed—all six hundred pounds of them—against his chest. The wind knocked out of him, of course, he opened his mouth, lost his prey (and his balance), and rolled down the steep incline, where he splashed into Hautête Creek's icy water while the yearlings split the kid three ways.

When the last bone of the young mutton had been ground into bear fodder, Dusty picked up a small morsel of white pelt and took it to Spooky, who was shivering and licking himself near the stream. When she waddled up and dropped the skin in front of him, he reached out with a huge paw, slowly rolled it over several times, then turned and licked her across the forehead.

Facing the realities of survival, the yearlings had taken hold of the principle of teamwork pursuant to offense and defense. As autumn whortleberries, corms, and grass sprouts disappeared, the team had poached more booty from other animals, intimidating every species except the grizzly from whom I had taught them to retreat. Their lake-country home in north-central British Columbia was an outback frontier, a biologically dynamic wilderness whose outward serenity was constantly violated by predation whenever and wherever hunger stalked. Beneath the beauty of each lingering sunset and forest glade prowled beasts of prey with sharp incisors and tremendous biceps. Those few intrepid early prospectors and trappers of the Hudson's Bay Company who had explored this region without opening it up for today's generation were of one accord in their reports, whose gist was: "It ain't no account for civilized homelife!"

In his own way, however, Spooky often demonstrated that the northland, with all its legacy of violence, suffered no lack of gentleness.

The first polar storm clouds rolled in on the tenth of November. Two days later, when the temperature dropped to thirty degrees below zero, the yearlings crawled into the hibernation shelter and fell asleep. There were no real thaws after that, but the winter months didn't seem as frigid as those of the previous year. The snow pack was on an average six to eight feet below normal, but no sudden changes occurred to inflict great damage within the forest. There was some ice-blasting, a condition of seventy-mile-an-hour winds which hurled tiny, sharp ice crystals, blasting them for hours against tree trunks, and removing the bark and cambium layers from those fringe trees exposed to the onslaught.

I read all the books I hadn't opened the previous year and spent a part of each day expanding my hurried diary entries of the summer months to include such indefinables as "reflection and evaluation." On one bright day in early March, I hiked across the lake to Larch's cabin to borrow a dozen of his books which I had declined to take earlier. Weather permitting, I snowshoed at least five miles a day to maintain my physical fitness. The bears rarely stirred that winter, even when the temperature inside the cabin went up to sixty-five degrees. They never once asked to go outside until April.

Larch was unable to get in with supplies until the fifteenth of May, at which time he flew in with a bush pilot. The two men left the following morning, since Larch had to return to Victoria. A powerful group in Prince George had by then begun to oppose the

game refuge on the grounds that it would close too
much government land to preemption and thus
perpetuate population deficiencies in that part of the
Dominion. Larch was even more silent, nervous, and
restless than he had been in October. The bears were
timid in his presence as if they regarded him as I
did—as a stranger.

On the fifteenth of July, more as an experiment
of the moment with the bears than as a serious ex-
plorations for future prospecting operations, I packed
a ten-day supply of food into the Trapper Nelson,
loaded Rusty and Scratch into the canoe—Dusty
wouldn't leave Spooky—paddled across the lake, and
hiked up into the eastern watershed of the Ominecas
above the Nation Lakes Basin. In addition to proving
that the bears would go where I went and were not
merely pastured to a specific range, I substantiated
Larch's theory that gold could be panned from most
of the Nation River's dendritic network of tributaries.
Without trails, the journey was extremely difficult,
especially when the route dropped below timberline
into practically impenetrable forest understory littered
with deadfalls.

As we picked our circuitous way through the timber
and over the shintangle ridges, every native species
of game stared at us in unhurried wonder. The spectacle of a man in the company of two large bears must
have been about as curious to the native animals as
was that primitive migration thousands of years ago
when ancestors of the Amerind first ventured south
through the same region.

Although laborious to approach because of the
luxuriant density of the riparian forest, the quartz-lined
stream beds yielded gold and platinum nuggets that
made my onerous Takla operations seem a ridiculous
waste of time and effort. The impasse, of course, was
that insurmountable problem of supplies which no
man could fly, float, or pack in, not to mention the
leaden weight of gold and platinum to back-pack
out.

As we crossed the lake returning home, I could see
Dusty and Spooky in good fettle sitting on the porch

surveying the lake. When we were within shouting distance, I called Dusty's name. She swam out to meet us with a demonstration of wild hilarity that came near capsizing the canoe. Spooky, true to form, disappeared.

Half running, half fluttering across the sand, two of the robins met us as we beached. As per custom, I cautioned the bears to sit perfectly still while I greeted the birds. Only two had returned to us that year, one cock and one hen.

Disillusioned and bitter, Larch came in unexpectedly by motor launch to spend the entire month of August. With both parents dead, with Parliament adjourned without a vote in favor of the reserve, and with no employment, he was a very silent, downcast, nervous man. In desperation I laid out a program of the most slavish physical work on the sluice box and long weekend hikes into the Ominecas which concentrated his thinking upon immediate goals. At night he would sit by the hour at the hearth with the bears or would walk alone down the starlit beach. His moccasined tread was so soft that I rarely knew when he returned to roll up in his blankets by the fireplace embers. I never forced conversation on him when he wanted to be silent. The north woods could heal their own.

When home from their forage, Rusty, Dusty, and Scratch would continually try to bamboozle Larch out of a chocolate bar, a box of raisins, or a belly-rub by lying on their backs and pawing the air, by bringing him their toys for a temporary loan, or by holding him down and licking his face. Physically, they were by then too strong for any human resistance.

That month we all enjoyed once more a shared period of eager companionship. It was again as if a great chunk had been gouged from the best part of our lives the day Larch left the lake.

12

Gunshot

If I could only end this story here in phrases of pure gratification, or turn back the days and nights to reverse certain events, how eagerly I would do so! But that is impossible; and since no part of this account is fictitious, I am compelled to relate, neither soft-pedaling nor exaggerating, all the circumstances in exact, chronological sequence, as they took place.

Before leaving at the end of August, Larch remarked, "Bob, I have never heard of a relationship between a man and an animal to compare with that between you and Rusty."

"It frightens me to the core, Larch," I said. "I can't give him up. He's three years old and capable of complete independence. I ought to get back home and finish college. But I simply can't give him up. A bear ought to roam day and night—aimlessly—especially here in the lake country where so many interesting things happen just over the next hill. Why don't they go on over that next hill? Why don't they make it easy for me and find a mate and go live with their own kind as I've planned from the first day I took them in?"

"Ponder it, my friend," he said. "Ponder it for two months and give me the answers to your own questions when I bring in your supplies toward the first of November."

Rusty became more and more reluctant to leave the area where I worked. On the first of September he allowed Dusty and Scratch to forage on their own. It was, of course, a source of concern to me to have

146

the two less aggressive bears afield without him. By the tenth of the month Rusty refused to forage at all unless I accompanied him. On the morning of the fourteenth, shortly after Dusty, Scratch, and Spooky had disappeared down the lake, Dusty returned to the sluice box where I was working. She was in a state of agitation bordering upon insanity. She whined, nudged me with her nose, then stood up and knocked me sprawling into the water. Rusty rushed in and the two bears engaged in a roaring fight in the middle of the creek until Spooky arrived and chased Rusty up a tree. Dusty ran over to the cabin steps, sat down, and began to moan. Dripping wet, I slowly approached and patted her on the head.

Things had happened so fast that I hadn't thought about Scratch. He had not returned with the other two bears. When I began calling his name, Rusty slid down from the tree and followed Spooky to the beach. Dusty ran after them. They all sat down after circling two or three times and looked back as if waiting for me to come along with them. The morning was gray, threatening rain, but I decided I'd best go along. Only by Indian pacing was I able to keep within sight of them as they headed south toward their forage range. When I lagged half a mile behind their lengthy strides, they turned and bellowed their impatience. Rusty ran back to see why I was so slow. There seemed little doubt that they were returning to the scene of some kind of trouble.

Four miles south of the cabin the bears left the beach and abruptly entered a thick lodgepole forest whose floor was disorderly with sphagnum-covered deadfalls and squaw wood. I remember how it smelled of fungus and rotting humus. Completely out of breath, I stumbled up a precipitous game trail to the crest of the hill where the timber was thinner.

There sat Scratch, moaning over a trapper's spring spike which was embedded above the fleshy part of his right heel. The trap's steel ring was attached to a chain which had been nailed to a log that lay between four trees. Even more cruel than the double-jawed toothed traps, those steel spikes were concealed in

game trails and were triggered by a spring which drove
their sharpened, barbed ends into the flesh too deeply
to be gnawed out. The sharpened ends came together
like a pair of ice tongs. Some trappers neglected to
spring these inhumane snares when they left the bush
in April, and all-too-common tragedies of painful,
terror-filled starvation occurred when animals un-
wittingly triggered the impaling steel. I have heard
trappers themselves denounce the spikes as one of the
cruelest devices ever invented by man.

I was not sure that Scratch would allow me to
approach and liberate him from the trap. I was not
even certain I could open the crescent-shaped spring
ratchet and pawl mechanism that held the barbs in
his leg. It looked rusty and much too complicated
to remove from a large, living animal. I even considered for a moment going back to the cabin for rope
to hog-tie the bear before attempting to remove the
trap. That would have meant an eight-mile round trip.
I decided to try first. As I sat down beside him and
grasped his muzzle for a nose shake, he moaned softly
and licked my face and hands. By rubbing his belly,
I got him to lie on his back so I could determine how
the trap worked. The foot itself was undamaged, but
I had no way of assessing the condition of the Achilles
tendon, bones, or nerves above the heel.

Some words Larch had spoken the year before came
back to me: "Fear's two offspring are panic and
courage." Scratch's own gentle responses helped me
overcome the seizure of shaking panic. Any courage
I gained was accidental. I cut and trimmed a strong
branch to insert between the curved spikes to depress
the spring mechanism. Speaking softly to the patiently
gurgling Scratch, who still lay on his back as if awaiting
surgery, I slowly placed the flat end of the trap between my boots and the log for maximum leverage.
The other bears stood in a circle and watched, with
the breathless attention of mounted museum specimens.
With one sudden forward yank on the pole, the spring
compressed and the two spikes opened with surprising
ease, causing Scratch but one violent thrust of pain
as they reversed through the flesh. When he jumped

backward with a shriek, he was free. The other bears growled savagely but didn't move.

Bleeding as he hobbled back to the cabin on three feet, Scratch stopped often, looked up into my eyes, and communicated his torture.

For three days and two nights he remained on the big bed where I brought him water and all the smoked fish he could eat. Having scrubbed the wound once with warm salty water, I did nothing further which might interfere with nature's own healing. I knew it would be useless without anaesthetic to try to sew the two open gashes. Scratch slept most of the time but tossed less when he could stretch his back next to mine; and when he could touch some part of Rusty's body, there was a soft purring to his breathing like that of a sunning lynx. On the third night he got up and limped away with Dusty and Spooky, tottering down the beach, undertaking to keep up with the pair who seemed to be trying to lose him.

During Scratch's convalescence, Rusty and I walked much of the range while Dusty and Scratch slept. Rather than walk alone, Rusty would return with me and forego a part of his meal. His full forage range was much greater than I could cover. I often hiked to the white limestone ridges north of Hautête Creek, hoping the bear would work the hundred-acre meadow below; but he also loved to sit there in the wind as though listening to the September songs of fir and hemlock that rose like deep-piped organ music from far below. At the same time he seemed to study all the skyline summits as if he planned to visit them some day.

Of all the ground Rusty and I covered together, I think his favorite activity—next to satisfying his interminable appetite—was canoeing. Nearly every afternoon in early October, when the wind would die down, I paddled up the Northwest Arm because there was no mistaking the pleasure he got out of the ride. With his remarkable sense of balance, he would sit for hours and steady the boat with his front paws on the gunwales while I paddled or fished. During those afternoons we achieved a kinship in which meanings required little physical vehicle for conveyance. I like to think we bridged at least a step in that mysterious, long-untrodden chasm between man and beast that has continued to widen as the centuries have slowly ticked away.

In the light of subsequent events, I lost all track of time toward the end of October. I neither recorded in my diary nor checked off the calendar days. After a day and night of icy drizzle, I remember a week of warm, sunny days and freezing nights. It was during this period of mild weather that all three bears suddenly resumed daytime foraging and came home to sleep away the chilly nights. As there had been no throb of float plane or outboard motor since Larch left, I assumed the lakes were now either game refuge or provincial park, otherwise I would have escorted the bears in directions away from the shoreline during the hunting season. Thus I was taken by surprise one morning when the veiled whir of a distant outboard filtered up the lake. Sounds carried, echoed, and altered over vast distances in the north woods, sometimes creating auditory illusions completely different from the true, original sound. On the morning in question I could have sworn I heard rifle reports as well as an outboard, but the disturbances were so far away and unsubstantial that I attributed them to crashing dead branches, which often fell at that time of the year.

"Just the same," I remember saying to myself, "I'll be glad to see those hulks come shuffling in."

At sundown the bears were not back. Total, moonless darkness settled over the woods and the eerie silence was more eerie because of the *noop-noop* call of a grouse who couldn't find her mate. In her anxiety, she revealed her position to a fox who dragged her away screaming. I sat on the stoop listening and waiting, jumping at every night call. At length the frost began to tingle the lobes of my ears and the end of my nose, so I went inside and built an extravagant fire. The bears would be half frozen when they arrived.

"Probably found a carcass belonging to some old grizzly and had trouble poaching it." I could see them climbing up on the bed, yawning in the warm room, circling half a dozen times for a spot before lying down, carefully avoiding the long down bag in the center because . . . "that was Bob's and he wouldn't surrender his place." At the slightest swish of the wind or snap of a freezing twig, I ran to the door and squinted into the black emptiness and listened. It was a nervous, wishful, worried reaction, because I knew the bears never approached the cabin on tiptoes; they raced in, rumbling and clouting one another as they pounded on the porch, wrestled for the right to open the slide bar, stampeded me for a greeting, then jockeyed for position on the bed or in the hibernation den, whichever struck their fancy of the evening. I sat throwing log after log on the fire until daylight, but the bears did not return.

At midmorning I ignited smoke fires, hoping to attract the occupants of an outboard which I thought I heard again downlake. I wanted to advise them of the tame bears they might see. After a lengthy walk down the beach without response, I returned to the cabin. The motor's monotone grew fainter as the boat apparently entered the channel of the Middle River. A plane with pontoons landed not far from Larch's cabin, and a second one seemed to descend somewhere below the mouth of the Driftwood River, at the upper end of Takla Lake's Northeast Arm. The two aircraft had been down but a few minutes when unmistakable rifle explosions began to reverberate among the peaceful hills.

Parliament had failed to issue a protective blanket of legislation.

I launched the canoe and paddled down the lake, keeping within a few feet of the shoreline to see if I could locate any traces of the bears. I had gone less than a mile when a choppy headwind whipped up two-foot waves that made canoeing impractical. Squally gusts reached into the unballasted, empty hull and spun the canoe around like a birch leaf. Losing freeboard as each icy wave broke over the bow and slopped gallons of water aboard, I pulled ashore, emptied the boat, and turned back toward home without a sign of the bears.

Two days later the forest became alive with flying squirrels gliding back and forth between trees as they sailplaned to earth, then raced back up the trees to repeat the peculiar performance as if it were a game. I hadn't known of their existence while the bears were around.

It was the third morning after their disappearance. I was searching the forest with binoculars when Rusty's weaving bulk appeared on the game trail. He was hurt. I called and ran to meet him, but when I was within fifteen feet, he stood erect, growled, and prepared to charge. When he threw his arms wide apart, claws up, I realized he was out of his mind and didn't recognize me.

"Rusty!" I shouted over and over as I backed away from his menacing snarls. He ignored me; in fact, he never looked me straight in the face, but rather seemed to search far over my head. The hair on his chest, shoulders, belly, and front legs was plastered flat with half-dried blood. There was no ascertaining the cause of his wounds. He growled fiercely, hackles so distended that he looked as if he had grown a shoulder roach like a grizzly. The bears snarled at almost everything; but when they growled deeply, they were prepared for combat. Rusty soon collapsed to the ground. After a brief struggle, he got up and wavered toward the cabin. I walked slowly after him, fully expecting him to turn on me at any moment. With pitiful groans of pain he climbed the steps, staggered into the cabin, crawled into the hibernation chamber he had used the two previous winters, and dropped in a sobbing heap. I was spared the ordeal of having to look into his glassy eyes, for he stared far beyond me as he snarled and hissed.

After removing the wooden lid, I took him a pan of water, but he flipped it across the room with a single swat of his right paw. I don't remember what I did

other than speak softly and try to think of something
I could bring him that he might remember. He merely
bared his teeth when I brought his old chewed up
blanket toy, but made no effort to remove the other
covers which I placed over him. His half-opened, un-
focusing eyes were glazed from lack of nictation; his
mouth, crusted with dried blood and froth, hung open
as he panted; his wrinkled tongue lay limp against
the floor. I tried to learn something of his wounds,
but his fur was too thick; and he was too crazed with
agony for any kind of examination. Overcome with
a feeling of absolute helplessness, I prayed for him
to lapse into unconsciousness so that I might be able
to determine the extent of damage and begin whatever
treatment I could.

If he had fought with a grizzly or a moose or a pack
of timber wolves over a carcass, I might hope for
recovery; but if that magnificent body carried a rifle
slug, there could be no prognosis. A cursory examination of his head and back revealed no scratches, no
missing clumps of hair; and for that reason my
heart sank. There was never a serious fight without
scratches and loss of hair. Once between panting groans
he turned over, at which time I had a passing look
at his chest. In the blood-matted fur I could see no
single source of bleeding; in fact, there appeared reason
to hope for no further loss now that he was home and
quiet.

During the long vigil that followed, I moved my
chair in order to be as close as possible to my friend.
As the hours slowly passed, he groaned and moved
less fitfully. At length he closed his eyes and dropped
into merciful sleep. I made no sound that would disturb
him.

I realized, as I had never before imagined, the
affection I shared with those bears. The thought kept
coursing through my head: "Where are Dusty and
Scratch—and Spooky? Why haven't they returned?
Have they ended as their mother did—in the bilge of
some hunter's boat?" They would have been such easy
prey to the riflemen; they would have rushed right
up in friendly enthusiasm, which the hunter, of course,

could later manufacture into a fabric of false adventure that would emanate glory about equal to that of shooting a neighbor's dog. I remembered the day Dan Yeager had given them candy.

Although numb to the passing of time, I knew by the light in the east when it was morning and by the darkness when it was night. While Rusty slept, I tiptoed to the fireplace where I prepared a large pot of oatmeal, mostly for him should he feel like eating when he awakened. After several cups of strong coffee and a pipe of tobacco when I felt like it, I would resume watch by the side of the hibernation shelter.

It was perhaps two or three days later, about midmorning anyway, when Rusty awakened. He was definitely weaker, but rational and almost his old, gentle, intelligent self as he looked up at me with a pained and puzzled expression in his big yellowish-brown eyes. When I reached over to pat him lightly on the head, he licked my hand with his old gratitude and affection. Within seconds I was inside the den next to him, holding his soft, troubled head next to my chest. He was soon asleep again with his head on my lap, his breathing more rhythmically even. He no longer groaned and twitched.

As he slept I recalled how the pitiful little creatures had splashed across Nugget Creek over on Babine Lake the day we first met, how they had clung to the high branches of the old fir until cold and hunger forced them to accept hospitality, how they had crept slowly but steadily into my life and for all practical purposes had made me almost one of their mind and world. I recalled the happy days of carefree cubdom we had loafed away near Red Fern's cabin before the fire. I could still see little Scratch pouncing upon Rusty or Dusty as they slept in the afternoon sun. He couldn't stand to see them sleep if he wanted to play. And when they clobbered him for the disturbance, he would run to me for protection. The sound of an outboard had meant so much fun when it brought Larch A-Tas-Ka-Nay to our shore that every time we heard an Indian launch on its way to or from Takla Landing we all rushed outside hoping for a visit from our friend.

What a cruel mocking irony! The very sound that had brought such delight now meant the wickedest tragedy for all of us.

As I sat there rubbing Rusty's soft, wooly head while he slept, I reflected upon the sensitivity of the so-called lower animals. How marvelously receptive most little animals are to the commands of their elders—not just to danger signals but to attitudes toward every activity. For those who have experienced the pleasure of watching an animal grow up, there is no end of amazement at the development of their increasing sensitivity. Present to a lesser degree in domestic creatures because of centuries of decreased responsibility—yet plainly there—the quotient of an animal's sensitivity to his natural surroundings and associates may be the rule by which we shall eventually appreciate his intelligence.

An hour before sunrise the next day, Rusty's breathing came more as long, irregular sighs through his open mouth. He didn't open his eyes. I laid his head on a folded blanket while I got up to light a candle and replenish the fire. Within five minutes I sat down beside him again to hold his head and speak to him. My friend was dead.

Trying to comprehend where I had failed those three wonderful, trusting animals, I was too shocked to move. Rusty had died by a single bullet through the small white spot on his chest. At first I assumed Dusty and Scratch had met a similar fate. It must have been around noon when at last I moved mechanically to the sluice box, got the pick and shovel, and dug the grave. I roped and dragged his heavy body to the sunny side of the cabin where we had spent so many hours in close companionship.

To make matters worse, the two robins, who had not yet migrated, stood on their shelf, watching silently during the burial.

Rusty and I were closest perhaps because I had leaned so heavily upon his early leadership with Dusty and Scratch. He was the quickest learner, the teacher and overseer of his brother and sister. During his third year he was the finest kind of companion, happy, eager, dependable, and loyal. As a dog knows, loves, and understands a master of his own choosing and invests his loyalty and devotion in that person, so Rusty blessed those precious months during which I was privileged to know him. As I carried big, round cobbles from Hautête Creek to cover his grave, I was careful not to step on the bear tracks in the mud between the creek and the cabin.

Still mentally numb that evening, I sat on the stoop to watch the dispassionate northland sunset. High cirrus strata picked up the red embers of afterglow over the Ominecas and reflected them on Takla's mirrorlike surface which produced the illusion of a double sunset. During no second of that vast, profound sweep of beauty were the bears out of my mind. They had taken intense satisfaction from the many dreamy twilights we had spent on that stoop, gazing beyond the shining lake and brooding forest to the crystal crags of the Divide.

The long intervening years have clouded neither the recollection of that companionship nor the sting of its loss.

On the following day, before beginning a compulsive search for Dusty and Scratch, I watched the robin population form a flock, circle several times above the cabin, then disappear in southerly flight over the timber.

13

The Indian's Story

Sometime during the night after Rusty's death, I became obsessed with a notion that Dusty and Scratch were not dead. I tried to recall the number of shots I had heard—six or eight, whatever a clip would hold. There might be blood on the sand or the hunters might have skinned a carcass on the spot. Only the most destitute Sekanis took bear meat for the table, because bears fed on carrion. Perhaps at least one of the bears had escaped. He or she might be at that moment wounded or lying helpless in some cave at the mercy of wolves or coyotes. I could postpone the search no longer.

At dawn I shouldered the Trapper Nelson packrack and rucksack and headed down the lake where I believed I had heard the shooting. As I walked slowly along examining every rock, every stick of ashen driftwood, every game trail that led to water, I was aware of many pairs of observing eyes. Frosty nights and nippy days were beginning to move elk, deer, and bighorn toward the Fraser River Valley, where they would spend the approaching winter. Wolves and lions, as momentary shadows, stalked the herds, while coyotes tailed the larger predators for the leavings.

Having covered in minutest detail the beach and its immediate riparian hem of glowing alders, poplars, and maples for five miles in fruitless search for spent cartridge cases, I began to work a discouraging way back home through the bunchberry and devil's claw understory of hilly forest. Like the well-trodden beach, any prints would have been obliterated by migrating ungulates. I saw no sign of *any* bear, neither tracks, ordure, nor forage patterns in bogs, meadows, or other favorite haunts. Backtracking was futile.

By the fireside that night two alternatives occurred to me: the bears had either been killed and hauled away, or fright—maybe gunshot wounds—had caused them to abandon the regular routes of their former forage ranges. Assuming at least one of them to be alive, I decided to follow Hautête Creek the next day for twelve miles up to Natowite Lake. There were "live" game trails on both sides of the stream, and that was the direction from which Rusty had returned. There were no signs of bear until I reached the lake.

Clearing out and repropping an ancient and crumbling lean-to of mossy logs, I made camp where Tochcha Lake Creek purled into Natowite Lake. Dark clouds kneaded and rumbled overhead. When the cold moderated, I covered the shelter with a tarp in preparation for a night of rain.

No sooner had I finished supper and bear-proofed my three-day food supply over a tamarack limb, than an old boar bear, overlayered with prehibernation blubber, barged into camp and tried to bluff me out of the lean-to by pounding the sod with his front paws, hissing, and exhibiting a set of yellow teeth much dulled by age and the habit of castanet champing during quarrels. The surest sign of a harmless bear was an initially grouchy disposition and a penchant for swagger and bluster. After swashbuckling around camp and threatening me through turbulent snarls and kicked-up duff, the old fellow got the message that I had been wised up long ago to the flimflam. When he started creeping up to where I sat under the shelter, something impelled me to rescue his dignity and self-respect by preventing him from crawling on his elbows and begging. Believing the smell of salt in my perspiration had attracted him in the first place, I poured out a tablespoonful of the precious crystals on a smooth rock. He continued to turn and lick the stone long after the last grain had been devoured. Subscribing to the belief that begging would defeat an animal—wild or domestic—exactly as it would a human,

I resorted to the most despicable subterfuge, even cruelty. Although the betrayal of his confidence burned a hole in my conscience—something no one forgets—I sprinkled a stone with pepper. The old bear sniffed, sneezed, and snorted, then raced to the icy creek where he plunged his head beneath the surface in an attempt to extinguish his discomfort. He never came near me again, nor would he forget the perfidy men stood for. That was precisely the point behind my otherwise reprehensible act; I was still reckoning with the assassination of my cherished friend whom I had so recently buried.

Drenched night and day by continuous downpour for nearly a week, and without the meagerest clue, I finally returned to the cabin, where I felt I might think more clearly. When the sky cleared, and warm southern chinooks brought Indian summer in early November, I packed a lunch every day and climbed the bare limestone minarets on both watersheds of Hautête Creek for high vigils above the alpine terraces where Rusty and I used to sit and contemplate the Ominecas. With binoculars I scanned over and over and over again every tree of every hillside; combed the shorelines of every palisade bench tarn; screened every bog, meadow, and barren where bearberries and morels were still available; followed every canyon, crest, and ravine. Mountain goats and Dall's sheep had dropped to timberline; elk, deer, and bighorn had already migrated. Grizzlies sat in the sun above the talus skirts guarding the caves where they planned to hibernate when the first polar storm swept south. Black bears prowled the ragged fringes of timberline, scrounging seeds and nuts hoarded beneath flagstone and shale by chipmunks and ground squirrels. Dusty and Scratch could not have been alive in that region and escaped detection. Returning to the cabin each night—a little more discouraged than the night before—I was tinkering with the idea of paddling down to Fort Saint James.

If I was to stay at Takla Lake, it was desperately urgent to chop fuel, catch and smoke fish, rechink the wall logs with fresh sphagnum, and reinforce the sagging roof; yet I could muster no desire to engage in any of these absolutely necessary activities. The nightly frosts began to drop to ten and fifteen degrees below zero. Trees were exploding in the mist-enshrouded forest. Cutting only enough wood and catching only what sockeye I wanted for my immediate needs, I pushed once again through all the old haunts along the former forage range, hoping for some clue that Dusty, Scratch, or Spooky might still be alive.

One breezy afternoon while I sat watching a stand of yellow poplars casting their moving reflections into the more somber shadows of hemlocks, the air suddenly filled with excited voices. Migrating V's of every species of waterfowl simultaneously took to the fly-ways. The annual mustering bivouac had crowded the shores and the water for a mile out on Takla Lake for a week; but I had never seen the region evacuate its total birdlife with such precipitate haste. Lone, ragged formations of trumpeter and whistling swans circled and soared for two hours before leading off toward the rice marshes of Minnesota. Ducks and geese honked incessantly for three days and nights as wave after wave formed flight patterns, positioned their decoys, then winged south.

Once the flock birds were gone; silence and serenity returned to the chilling north woods. Nonmigratory solitaires and ouzels whistled softly as they bobbed up and down as if doing push-ups on rocks in the creek.

The little hermit thrush, who sang throughout the summer and autumn from the cabin rooftop the prettiest tune in Canada, dropped from the gable, dead for no reason I could understand. Five minutes before he fell, I listened to his final, and perhaps most beautiful song. What a glorious way to go!

Gradually the evenings became too frosty of a twilight to sit on the stoop and watch the lake trout leap for caddis flies, making very pleasant sounds as they slipped back into the water. The raucous whisky-jacks and the chickadees with their rusty little squeaks were discreet enough to keep still when the wolves, the real minstrels, performed.

Late one afternoon I sat picking catclaw stickers out of my arms and legs and contemplating the remaining autumnal animals, most of whom were earning a living side by side in complete trust and mutual respect now that the bears, martens, and fishers were inactive. Red squirrels were hidden in sleep for the season, but flying squirrels seemed to be making up for all the gleeful soaring they had missed earlier, and most of my last two pounds of oatmeal went into fat-pouched little cheeks as some of nature's most perfect gliders learned to alight on my hat, back, and shoulders with a touch so delicate that the diminutive hitchhikers could almost land without my being aware of them except for their sassy collar-tugging for more cereal.

With the last throbbing thorn removed, I was about to go inside to grill a steelhead when the sputter of an outboard seemed to come from the dark, blue-green masses of spruce and cedar on Larch's side of Takla. I dreaded facing him or any other Indian, knowing how they felt about bears. I was prepared to ask him to take me down the lake. Somehow the boat didn't look like Larch's, yet no one else in the region knew I was there. All the propark Beavers had been forced out or burned out of British Columbia by the antirefuge Indians; so I imagined it to be a hunter seeking shelter for the night after having discovered Larch's cabin padlocked. An ironclad code—unwritten—of the northlands decreed that a person's cabin was always his and safe from invasion regardless of circumstances or eminent domain as long as it had a padlock on the door. Many cabins rotted and caved in from lack of upkeep because no one knew who the owner was, yet ethics precluded their preemption. When the boat reached midlake, I saw through the binoculars a single Indian hunched forward to protect his face against the freezing southwesterly. I rushed in to stoke the fire and begin supper for my guest, whoever he might be. I knew it wasn't Larch because the boat was piled too high with boxes, and Larch never used the Hudson's Bay bateau.

With the open smile of the lake country, the handsome young Indian threw me his fore painter, then cut the engine and docked alongside the drift-log landing. As the wind promised to rise during the night, we decided it would be safer to beach the craft rather than risk its pounding against the jetty.

"Names's Mark," he said as we shook hands. Indians rarely mentioned last names up here. On the way to the cabin he told me he was a Tahltan from Palisade Lake, north of Bear Lake and about a hundred miles beyond the upper end of Takla. He had been to Fort Saint James for certain winter supplies unavailable at the trading post at Takla Landing. Now engaged in placer activities, he had formerly trapped with Larch when the two men ran combined lines for seventy-five miles between Tochcha and Tsayta lakes.

"We're finished with that business of trapping," he said. "Earn almost as much making birch snowshoes up here in winter. Good cabin to hibernate in at sixty below. Pretty, plumb Sekani squaw—good cook. Pan gold in summer."

Before we entered the cabin he turned and asked, "How are the bears?"

I invited him in and related the story.

"By jingo, I'll bet those were the three I saw on my trip downlake. They were swimming across the lake to come out near Larch's cabin. A pair of three-year-olds and an older boar."

Dusty and Scratch would have associated the good times we knew over there with a security worth swimming five miles for after they saw what happened to Rusty.

"Did you hear anything at Fort Saint James?"

"Some Yank claimed he took a pot shot at three bears who looked like they might swim out to his boat. There was a big black boar and those younger bears. Said he was sure he hit one that had a white spot on his chest. Bear just stood there after he was hit and turned his head from side to side like he was talking to the man. Said he hit another one that pitched and fell but got up and limped away. Emptied a clip at their fannies, by jingo, as they disappeared in the underbrush. Do those sound like your bears?"

For a moment I was too stunned to speak.

"Beyond a doubt," I said. "To those bears a boat meant a fun ride, fishing, a deep-water swim." At least I knew what happened. "Tomorrow I'll paddle across if the wind lets up."

After supper we sat before the fireplace smoking out pipes and hating nearly everybody.

"Larch is now a game warden for the British Columbia Game Commission," Mark announced. "Operates out of Fort Saint James. Asked me to drop by and tell you they failed to get a bill passed through Parliament to make the lake country a sanctuary for wild animals. Guess you found that out the hard way. Hudson's Bay Company and the Department of Parks and Recreation got beat down by lumbering, mining, trapping, and sporting people.

"Too much trouble among Indians around Babine. Nobody happy over there any more. Mill's been burned to the ground twice. Some come right out and say the fires were set because the Northwest Lumber Company, Limited, took the strongest stand against the park bill and brought in Kitamats after firing Babines and Beavers."

Before leaving, Mark left me thirty pounds of moose jerky and twenty pounds of sausage and pemmican. "Larch sent this," he said. "He'll be in with supplies as soon as he can get three or four days off. By jingo, why don't you come to Palisade Lake and spend the winter with me? Couple o' good squaws left on upper Takla."

"Thanks, Mark. I'd like that. Depends on what I find on the other side of the lake. I may even thaw out my bones in Southern California this winter—down where they grow oranges and dates and figs."

"I had an orange once. Best damned thing I ever ate."

As loggers used to say, two "drizzerable" days of sullen wet wind blew by before I dared risk the open lake in the canoe. To mollify my impatience, I spent the time rechinking the cabin logs, rebracing roof members, and chopping wood, should I decide to spend another winter there.

Without wind, the crossing was uneventful. Bear tracks were everywhere in the vicinity of Larch's cabin—one set about fourteen inches long and two sets about ten. I called and whistled until I was hoarse, ran for hours up and down the beach, and climbed the dark red shale canyon for two miles toward the divide. Without a fresh sign, I returned, unlocked the cabin, and began supper. The pungent smell of sprucewood smoke, beans, onions, and coffee might bring them in, I thought. After nightfall the northland settled into a strange, absolute silence, as if the Canadian autumn darkness itself were a muffler of sound.

Ordinarily, even beneath the deep, fifty-below-zero lid of winter, I was a dawn riser; yet for some reason, perhaps utter exhaustion from the mental and physical drain of the preceding weeks, the morning was almost gone when some carefully soft scratching and low whining at the door awakened me. In a bound I was out of the sleeping bag and tugging at Larch's door, which always stuck a bit due to an outside fringe of moosehide weather stripping.

Balanced on his haunches, pawing the air with both front feet like a hungry poodle, squawling like a prodigal collie, sat my dear friend Scratch. Throwing my arms around the bear, I bellowed, moaned, cried, and laughed until I was numb from the cold. I finally coaxed him into the warm interior. As I had done that first morning after his foster mother had consigned him to me on Babine Lake, I cooked a large pot of porridge into which I stirred half a pound of oleomargarine, a cup of brown sugar, and three cans of evaporated milk from Larch's emergency stock. I could hardly wait until after breakfast to head for the forest.

Betting all my chips on Scratch's natural inclination to follow a scent trail to rejoin Dusty and Spooky, I threw a few things into the Trapper Nelson and allowed Scratch to lead wherever he might. Without any preliminary exploration or hesitation, he picked up a scent like a basset and started up the canyon toward the Pacific Divide. He still limped from the slow-healing trap wound but apparently was unhurt otherwise.

The day was crisp and frosty. Some of the vapor from my breathing froze into little round icicles on my beard, while the fur on Scratch's chest and shoulders froze solid white and we puffed out billowing breath clouds along the miles of dark, frozen shadows up the canyon trail. After a fifteen-minute rest at noon, we climbed on to the summit, which we reached late that afternoon.

We were descending the other side of the pass when Scratch suddenly stopped and sat on his haunches. When I sat down beside him and put my arm around his neck, he nuzzled my ear. An open bog lay about half a mile above the basin which cradles Purvis Lake. Two bears emerged from a willow thicket and began digging quamash tubers on the sward side adjacent to the stand of leafless shrubbery.

When he scented our approach, Spooky sprang erect and swung his head toward us. Dusty stood up momentarily, then disappeared into the thick willow brake. Favoring their front legs or shoulders, both bears limped pitifully.

Although I called to her and sent Scratch into the thicket after her, Dusty limped away as fast as she could, following Spooky toward the dense spruce and lodgepole hills south of the lake. In about an hour Scratch returned to where I was sitting on a deadfall at the side of the trail below the bog.

He followed me back to Larch's cabin, but I had the feeling he did so with reluctance.

14

Double-Bitted Ax

Scratch and I sat in front of Larch's big fireplace until late that night. As I rubbed his head and scratched his ears and chin, I reviewed Dusty's situation. Thanks to all those early forage walks and good food, she was about able—with Spooky's help—to live independently of man. Her weight, speed, and strength would be respected by every contemporary except the grizzly in the forest, and her wound would inspire a wide arc of no-man's-land wherever she roamed. There was no animal quite as dangerous as a wounded bear. Although I was not satisfied about the wound, there was nothing I could do. My decision was to return to my cabin, leaving Dusty and her mate—and Scratch if he wanted to stay—with their fears of perfidious man.

The next morning while packing for the return trip across the lake, I saw Scratch rush away toward the canyon as if returning to his kind. Unwilling at first to accept his decision, I had almost gotten hold of my reason through the convincing argument that such was nature, and so much better for Scratch since I could not continue nursemaiding even one bear indefinitely. Slowly he slipped back to the edge of the clearing—with Dusty. Both bears stopped when I called. Scratch licked Dusty across the nose, then loped over and boarded the canoe. Dusty limped back into the canyon for a few steps, stopped, looked at Spooky who was sitting in the middle of the trail fifty yards above, then sniffed toward Scratch and me as I paddled away from the shore.

The succeeding week was a feverish rush from daylight to dark to beat the inevitable arctic blasts that were already well on their way. I had made almost no preparations for winter. As I sawed, split, and back-packed dry wood, spun lures across the mouth of Hautête Creek and reeled in two hundred steelhead and rainbow trout, smoked the catch, and securely hung it in the food cache, Scratch was always nearby. When the fish weren't biting, I returned to harvesting wood. The bear was satisfied with short evening walks, because he was through with serious eating for the season. In due course I found myself looking forward to winter again and the occasion when Larch would come in with supplies.

During those late autumn days, Scratch, like Rusty, was interested in everything around him; yet at the height of that interest in a flying squirrel, a pica, a diving osprey, a passing moose, he would still in-variably sit down and scratch one ear, then the next, as if thinking it over. Each day I became more stricken with the idea that I had neglected that bear because of the powerful influence exerted by Rusty's out-standing personality. Scratch possessed none of Rusty's fierce independence and driving will; but he was gifted, on the other hand, with a gentleness and meekness akin to humility. I followed Rusty; Scratch followed me. And that was the difference. Affectionate and playful as a cub, Scratch's traits of dependence superseded a bear's natural tendency to roam in-dependently of every other living creature. In front of the fire he would roll, play with his toes, chew a stick of cordwood, or assume ridiculous positions on the floor to flag my attention when I got drowsy. If I dozed, he nibbled my ears; if I failed to register an expression of applause to any of his antics, he repeated the performance until I did. Scratch understood more human words and physical gestures than Rusty or Dusty. More were necessary with Scratch. From cubhood he had always led me to what he wanted me to see, or shown me what he wanted, by pointing with his nose, while the other two would just skip it if too much effort was involved or if it seemed unimportant to make me understand.

On the sixth day after the trip across the lake, Scratch and I were walking down the lake shore toward the bog when he stopped short, lifted his nostrils, champed his teeth, then plunged into the twelve-foot-tall underbrush of alder and willow above the beach. Within moments of his noisy sortie, I saw Dusty and Spooky emerge across the bog with Scratch at their heels. That pair of wounded bears had swum the icy, five-mile channel for the second time!

I was frankly desolated to see them back. The Purvis Lake region along the eastern watershed of the Divide was beyond even the most avid hunter and would have been an ideal range. At first I attributed their return only to the fact that Dusty had seen me paddle away with Scratch and that she missed him enough to swim the lake in order to be with him occasionally. Once more I feared my interference—despite the best of intentions—would only harm the bears' own balance. Rifle reports from the vicinity of Larch's cabin, however, seemed to indicate more pragmatic reasons for their having swum the lake twice.

Call and coax as I might, Dusty painfully remembered man's treachery each aching step she took; and nothing Scratch and I could ever do would overcome what the man with the rifle had accomplished. Had I been able to make them understand, I would have taken them to the Purvis Lake cabin for hibernation. I could have slipped away after they were asleep, and they would have been on their own. Even had the move been possible, however, there was no assurance that instinct would not have returned them to Hautête Creek, pleasant memories of which must have lingered in their minds from their recent cubhood.

I was reminded of my mother's words: "All hunting, except for survival, is a shabby postponement of growing up, and any claim that shooting one of God's wild creatures is sportsmanlike should receive the same condemnation as bullfighting, bearbaiting, dogpitting, or cockfighting."

If Dusty ever came near the cabin, I never knew

it for sure, although there were times when I seemed to sense her proximity. After the shooting, the sight of me frightened her. Spooky had no doubt communicated to her what he had feared all along about man. They would never forget what they had seen and felt the day the bullets ripped into them, yet it pained me each time I saw her limp away in the distances as if she felt *I* were that hunter.

Scratch's native timidity and tendency to run at the first sign of danger had probably saved him a bullet wound, but that characteristic of his also had other implications. Like those of all timid bears I have ever known, the outer sides of his eye sockets slanted upward a bit like those of an oppossum. According to northern Indians, that made him a natural night prowler, unsure of himself in the daylight. As a three-year-old he became more and more clumsy, losing his earlier dexterity in climbing trees and walking fallen logs. Alone, he wouldn't engage in those keen-witted escapades the three had formerly employed to filch a grizzly's cache or to intimidate a mountain lion away from its prey. On one of our walks he even underwent a paddle-tail thrashing when he passed over the lodge of a colony of beavers at the edge of their private pool. His growing reluctance either to defend himself against aggressors or to assume the offensive in the procurement of a balanced diet could become matters of serious concern following hibernation. Only the fierce could earn a living in that highly competitive forest. Once again I dared consider the zoo.

On the afternoon of November fifteenth I heard two launches on the lake, one going north, one south. At a point about opposite Larch's cabin, both boats arced in toward Hautête Creek. Arriving together, Mark from the north and Larch from the south, the two Indians beached their crafts side by side.

"By jingo, you sure came today!" Mark said to Larch as they shook hands.

"I thought about you all day, Mark," Larch replied. "I had the feeling you'd be here."

Although both Indians swore their arrival together was what they called "simultaneous dual performance"—a Nadene belief related to extrasensory perception, I had every reason to believe they had planned to meet at my cabin on the fifteenth.

With my new supplies and equipment unloaded and properly stored, we prepared an early dinner in order to have an uninterrupted walk down to the creek where I had enjoyed recent good luck in the sluice box. Scratch seemed to be equally fond of Mark and Larch, lending some support to the old saying that "bears and some Indians hibernate together."

"I'll believe it," I said, "if either of you can coax Dusty in."

"Not me," Larch replied. "She's not very happy at the moment, but she's where she belongs."

"Me neither," Mark agreed. "But I'll take Scratch when you decide you can't live without those oranges. I'll take him to Palisade Lake. No hunters, no trappers. Just good friends and plenty to eat."

"Give me six months, Mark, to decide on that."

"I'll pick him up in May. Meantime, let's enjoy the autumn air. It seems to me that only leaves possess the secret of a beautiful death."

As we sat around the fire for the next two evenings, Mark told of the wonders of the Palisade Lake country. He opened a drawstring leather pouch and poured out onto the table a pound of large gold and platinum nuggets. He had yarns of sockeye and rainbow, of game and wild berries, of the garden of carrots and rutabagas that his squaw cultivated. He amused us with Tahltan legends concerning the dehorning of mosquitoes, of digging glaciers for ice worms and mushroom roots, of dehydrated water tablets for traveling light in time of drought, and of various sagamore formulas "to keep from getting caught in the shadow of the sun!"

Larch, on the other hand, was more serious than he had been before the park issues turned out the way they had; but by virtue of the struggle, he had attained new philosophical stature. As Deputy District Game Warden he was in a position in which he could serve men and protect the wildlings he loved. On the day before returning to Fort Saint James, however, he revealed a further dimension to the tragedy of the bears, a double-edged blade of irony, even worse from our standpoint than every other aspect of the shooting.

"Bob," he said as we walked down the trail toward the cabin, "I hate to tell you this, but I have to. There is no further closed season on bear. Goes for the whole province; so hunters can come in here any time and start blasting away."

I wished I had never heard that shocking revelation. Right there I told Mark to come and get Scratch on May fifteenth.

Four days following the departure of Mark and Larch, the unusually long Indian summer came to a sudden close. Mark had brought a pair of the fine-webbed snowshoes with upturned toes, the kind he made and sold. It was so much easier to cross the un-packed drifts of fine powder with his product than with my commercially manufactured shoes, which were more like tennis rackets. Five yards beyond the cabin door the silently falling white mass blotted out the rest of the world for ten consecutive days. The only difference between night and day was the milky light that filtered through the frosted window panes when I opened the shutters after shoveling the snow away from the outside walls. Even with a continuous blaze in the fireplace, the glass panes frosted on both sides and had to be scraped daily.

Long ago the Tahltans and Sekanis discovered that the temperature in the snow-well around the base of a tree was often forty degrees warmer than, say, half-way up the trunk; therefore, when they maintained deep "wells" around their cabins, a thermometer under the gables would rarely register lower than ten degrees below zero even when it was fifty below at the top of the "cell." Under the most extreme conditions, it never took more than an hour a day to shovel out the "well" and pack the banks, thus economizing on fuel and candles inside. Using a bright reflector and rigid frugality, I was never able to do with fewer than three hundred twelve-inch candles per winter.

Scratch refused to enter the hibernation cell where Rusty had died, because I was unable to scrub all the smell of blood and urine away; so I boxed in the table on three sides, hinged a door on the fourth, and lined the cavity with a dozen old Army blankets. Larch had brought over all his bedding. The bear purred his delight from the moment the new den was finished.

On New Year's Day he first emerged when a pack of six timber wolves assembled just outside the cabin door for a serenade. He clawed the door to go out and join them; but since timber wolves are notorious for digging fat three-year-olds out of hibernaton for a feast of bear meat, I bribed him to remain inside and share a smoked steelhead with me. Between January fifteenth and March fifteenth he awoke regularly once every two weeks, drank a can of condensed milk, ate half a smoked trout, and sat in front of the fire with me for sometimes two hours with his head on my knees.

Between December and March the bear left the cabin but twice, once on a brilliant day in January when we walked down to the lake to listen to the final cannonading and watch the momentary rainbows in exploding showers of ice splinters as the surface underwent complete freezing. Scratch accompanied me in late February when the old dead spruce on the hill south of the cabin crashed and split longitudinally. A living tree would never have accumulated such an unusual weight of ice and snow. The great shell enriched our larder with thirty-five pounds of amber honey. At forty below zero we had to wait only five minutes for all the freshly exposed bees to become totally inactive and for the honey to congeal into a solid, nonsticky mass which I chopped from the wooden shell with a hatchet. Scratch for the first time in his life refused honey, but he must have eaten two thousand bees.

Our winter was a relaxed, quietly thoughtful time when I could read for uninterrupted hours the stacks of books and magazines Mark and Larch had delivered, or, weather permitting, I could hike a mile out on the lake and watch the rosy alpenglow on the snowy peaks under circumstances never possible during any other season. I still swallowed hard at times when I thought of the open season on bears. Somewhere out there in a cave, under a wickerwork of logs or in a hollow cottonwood, lay Dusty, sorely wounded, disillusioned each time she awoke and discovered she was not in the cabin with her two brothers.

I quote from a diary entry dated January 1 of that year:

"As roads are built into the lakes and outboards become more available, and government lunacy abets the outrage, man will obliterate this wild community, not fully understanding the reason for his destruction. It is not important that a hawk takes a robin, that a bear robs a grouse nest. That's nature's own salient way even if we don't understand it. Our robins lived no life of fear when the hawk was gone, and the grouse laid a new clutch. Wilderness life has gone on that way since the beginning, and the prey has withstood predation. But when man steps in, be it to raise a set of triplet bears or to seize trophies to satisfy a lingering Neanderthal cry for booty, the very soul of nature cringes for having endowed one of her creatures with intelligence disproportionate to responsibility."

From the low, southeast sunrise until midafternoon sunset in the southwest, I spent my customary five hours out of doors at vigorous activity: hiking, sawing up and splitting the fallen bee tree, and keeping holes open through the ice on the lake for fresh trout. To prevent refreezing or losing the openings each time it snowed, I erected twelve-foot tripods of spruce saplings and thatched the resulting "teepees" with green boughs. To keep the fishing lines from freezing, I simply left them in the water. When fishing, I ran from hole to hole to check the lines, because it was much too cold to remain more than five minutes in one place despite my heavy goosedown parka, knee-length moose moccasins worn inside thick leather mukluks, and woolen mittens inside two-ply mooseskin gauntlets.

One day in February I was trudging back to the cabin with twenty pounds of rainbow trout when two middle-aged Indians driving a dog team began to shout my name.

"We're from Takla Landing. Forty mile," one man named Rupert said as they approached the cabin. "Mark, he my good friend. You Mark's friend, you my friend. He say we go bring moose quarter come February. Throw damn fish to dogs!"

"Come on inside and we'll build a feast and smoke the calumet," I said after tossing my hard-earned catch to the snarling, underfed, trundle-tail curs as the Indians unhitched them. The dogs would not allow me to come near even to hand them food. "Where can we put the dogs?"

"Dogs never go inside," said the Indian whom Rupert called Crow Face. "Dig cave in snow well. Your bears asleep?"

"I have only one bear left, and he is asleep."

Both men shook their heads either in disbelief or disgust when they peeped through the door under the table. Too drowsy to emerge, Scratch barely looked up. Before beginning the meal, I climbed down into the cellar and brought out twenty pounds of unfrozen smoked trout, cut it up, and took it out to the dogs. The Indians considered the act one of rash extravagance, but I was thinking in terms of prime ribs of moose au jus, a warm dry cabin, and a comfortable bed instead of a "cave in snow well."

Although these men were in frequent contact with the outside world over the waves of radio as well as a caterpillar and sled road which fed into the trading post of Takla Landing, they were unable to fill me in on any kind of news other than exorbitant local speculation on the "dizzy mucklark living with bears on the Northwest Arm."

During their two-day visit I could not help comparing Rupert and Crow Face to men like Red Fern, Larch, and Mark. I was extremely grateful for the two hundred pounds of fresh meat they had brought as well as for their cheerful, considerate companionship. They were men of good will and emotional maturity as far as I could judge; yet they interpreted Mark's and Larch's way of life—not to mention mine —in a sinister and superstitious fashion. The point of their sermons, couched in no subtle undertones between the lines, was summed up by Rupert:

"When man quit peltin' for pannin', all the same man hibernate with bear!"

His message was that any cooperative feast between man and the "lower" animals was a sign not necessarily of weakness so much as one of loss of dominion. To these men, the Catholic missionary's committee of three little gods—"Some guy with his son and a spirit nobody understands . . ."—seemed to be constantly losing petty brushfire struggles with warty little devils.

"Man always in the middle, catch hell from both sides," said Crow Face. "Missionary god always losing money, needs help from man. What kinda god needs help from man? No good when Nadene take on white man's ways."

Neither man could read or write, yet each was a veritable thesaurus of ancient lore passed from generation to generation around the hearth fires of evening. They thumbed through my magazines, giggling at photographs advertising the latest civilized necessities.

Crow Face added, "My father say book steal man's ideas and replace them with thoughts of other man you can't look in the eye."

Rupert had a captivating yarn to spin about some of the Babine Indians at Topley Landing who had lost their jobs at the mill. At least a part of the gold Peter A-Tas-Ka-Nay's crew had panned out of Hautête Creek had gone toward "salting" placer claims on the hill above Topley village. Many imported Kwakiutls and Kitamats had quit their new jobs during the height of the rush season, had purchased—at ridiculous prices—the fraudulent claims from the Babines, then had been obliged to thumb rides back to the coast when starvation began to set in. Rupert implied that a certain R.C.M.P. constable not only refused to arrest the Babines, but that he might have thimblerigged the whole caper.

Before leaving, the men beeswaxed the runners of their sled and the slender moosehide harness with the new wax I had rendered from the windfall. A swirling norther with fifty-mile-an-hour gusts began whipping down from the Beaufort Sea as they mushed the dogs out onto the frozen lake against a roiling wall of blackened blizzard. I implored them to remain until the storm had passed, but they just laughed at the idea. Only a white man would allow a simple inconvenience like cyclonic weather to influence his movements. They expected to reach Takla Landing within ten hours.

For days after the two Indians had gone, the words of Charley Thwaite kept coming back to me: "Man can't live like a bear. A bear can't live like a man."

15

The Final Silence

As the days grew longer in March, I did everything I could to hold back the clock. Scratch came out of hibernation gentler and more devoted than ever, and almost hourly I regretted my promise to surrender him on May fifteenth. To lengthen the days with the bear, I took to rising before sunrise and retiring around midnight. With southwesterlies and early thaws, the snow disappeared on southern exposures within a fortnight, and the unrestrained annual miracle of growth unfolded with an intemperance of fragrance not often experienced in the somber, thrifty north woods. Pausing only long enough to enjoy the saprophytic snow plants in the deep forests where the snow hadn't yet melted, I spent every possible daylight hour on sunny slopes and meadows where trillium, cassiope, and pickernel were in flower. At night we sat on the stoop and listened to the roar of Hautête Creek which reached a twelve-foot crest of revolving mud and mica because of the sudden thaw that was flushing the canyons of the Natowite watershed. Knowing we were sitting there, the six big timber wolves still commanded the trail between the cabin and the mooring jetty. Their ancestral tunes, I must confess, in the springtime sounded like rehearsals for an amateur hour. Scratch nudged me with his nose and flattened back his ears as the wolves' deep-throated notes rose and fell, but he made no effort to leave the stoop. Both species maintained a quiet but armed truce.

I was awakened during the first week of April by pine grosbeaks and hermit thrushes who had weathered every seasonal tempest to keep ther annual date of arrival. Mountain bluebirds, swallows, and whip-poorwills dipped high and low to sweep the air of insects. Mallards, pinetails, mergansers, canvasbacks, teal, baldpates, and buffleheads gossiped all night after their successful return to the northland, while loons cackled and bitterns sounded as if they were thumping a kettledrum. Swans, brant, and snow geese held reedy, high-pitched arguments over feasts of fry and insect larvae pouring into the lake from the raging Hautête. Twelve-pound cohoe surfaced for five hundred yards around the creek's outlet as numerous schools of the big salmon prepared to enter when the water cleared. Whistling clouds of stormy petrels passed overhead without stopping.

Scratch led the way down the beach to the bog as soon as new shoots of skunk cabbage revealed underground niches of succulent rhizomes. He was never clumsy at scooping up chipmunk-sized lemmings and voles whose busy corridors crisscrossed every lowland bog and meadow. These prolific rodents generally denuded most meadows by the middle of summer every year. I never learned where they went after eating themselves out of pasture, but they always showed up in the spring with large families. Hawks, owls, and every mammal predator from the tiniest masked shrew (one fifth the size of a lemming) to mountain lions moved onto the meadows when the voles and lemmings appeared. We never observed them in upland sward above timberline.

As the throb of life returned to the Takla region each Easter, and delicate fawns and kids sniffed calypso orchids and shooting stars, I was always awed at the forces of violence associated with the nominally gentle springtime. As the earth spun into the vernal equinox, the jet stream of upper air currents flattened near the poles, often producing the traditional "March winds and April showers." In the north woods, as on the plains of Alberta and Saskatchewan, the ferocity of these winds could be fully understood only after seeing an osprey glide inadvertently into an updraft which ripped out or crimped enough wing and tail feathers to plunge him dead into a lake or against a mountain crag.

In early April fingery cloudlets collected around the peaks and mushroomed within minutes to heady, sky-filling "tar babies" charged with sufficient electricity to whittle glaciers, reshape the summits of mountains, shatter limestone cliffs, and split five-hundred-year-old hemlocks into matchwood. The roar of avalanching snow from ten-thousand-foot hanging cornices was at times indistinguishable from the bombardment of thunder during the great reverberations of the first half hour of those storms. As the wind and barometer dropped, the temperature always moderated, and the nice, hospital-like smell of ozone pervaded the air. Once electrical equilibrium had been established between earth and cloud country, and all static charges had been grounded, the ensuing downpour would acquire a violence all its own, not unlike the notorious flash floods characteristic of the southwestern United States. I always felt giddy when caught in one of those

April storms, as if the lively ozone had addled me a bit.

How marvelously nature coached most of her creatures—even bears and squirrels—to leave the timber during an electrical squall! By habit I used to rush to trees that had just been struck, hoping to rescue any nestlings thrown to the duff by the impact. Without exception, the ones I found were dead.

Scratch and I were hiking down the beach after a day and night of confinement by a late April storm when the bear suddenly sat down on my feet as was his habit when he didn't want me to proceed. I had been thinking of the owl who had called and called on the night before, yet received no answer. The Tahltans avowed that an unanswered owl was bad luck. From a small clearing above the six-foot bank came the most forlorn wailing I have ever heard. It sounded like a wolf mourning over a trapped and dying mate. Not wishing to commit the indiscretion of violating his privacy, I eased up to the bank and peeped over. To my horror there sat Spooky, moaning, muzzle pointed to the sky. On the glistening wet grass in front of him lay Dusty—dead.

When he scented us, he limped away, still crying, and I never saw him again. Running to Dusty's torn and battered form, I found her neck broken and chewed open; great chunks of fur and flesh lay scattered about the clearing. There had been a hideous struggle. In the muddy gumbo wash nearby were the unmistakable tracks of a sow grizzly. And so, Dusty, like Rusty, actually met her death at the hand of the hunter. From the first time I saw her limp, I feared she would be unable either to run, defend herself, or climb a tree if she should encounter a belligerent sow grizzly.

I wouldn't leave her there for the wolves and coyotes to tear apart and devour, so I went back to the cabin and got a shovel. Scratch moaned as Spooky had until I covered her grave with cobble like Rusty's. We sat silently on the mound until nearly noon. I was still wondering—as I had indeed wondered throughout the winter—how much better off the bears would have been had I not interfered.

By May first I had enough gold to realize at least a part of my dream. But the floods along the watersheds of the lake's tributaries brought tempting new placer which I sluiced and panned on clear afternoons when Scratch wanted to lie in the sun and study my peculiar streamside activity. When he wanted to forage even the most distant range—four, six, eight miles from the Hautête—I trudged along with him; although I noted that if I made a move toward home, he was at my heels.

Scratch had become a very serious bear during his fourth year. By the first of May he weighed at least four hundred pounds and stood five feet eight inches tall when sudden bursts of exuberance prompted him to plant a clumsy paw on my shoulder and give my face a thorough licking. He was too strong by then for me to escape his massive hug without uttering the "No!" signal, which I held in reserve for emergencies. Outward displays were serious business with that bear; and if I laughed at any of his several rough techniques or if my enthusiasm lagged behind his, he simply drew back and knocked me to the ground where he piled on top of me.

From the earliest days of our association the three cubs had gently nibbled my nose, ears, and fingers to get my attention. They employed the same artful devices as expressions of endearment and as a sure-fire means of changing the subject under circumstances of embarrassment to them. During the slow, day-by-day growing-up process, the burly hulks had become such a familiar part of the household that they no longer seemed unusual in the cabin. They were so gentle indoors. Thus, however absorbed I might be in a book, a chore, or simply in reflection, the lick of a rough tongue or the cinch of rubbery lips on fingers, earlobes, or nose was natural and expected.

The original bargain with my conscience to raise the bears and then return them to their native habitat when they were equipped to earn their own, normal way had not reckoned sufficiently with the element of animal devotion. With an almost British lack of sentimentality, I had felt sorry for three cute little teddy-bear orphans, offered them temporary food and protection, trained them to meet their own responsibilites. Then, out of the finest kind of obedience, respect, trust, compatibility, and affection, there had grown a depth of mutual friendship far beyond anything I could have believed possible at the time the cubs arrived.

As the day approached when I would have to say good-bye to Scratch I couldn't bring myself to the gradual, systematic weaning I had planned. As we walked beneath the balsams or leaned into the delicious wind on the crestline meadows, I dreaded more and more the idea of giving him up; yet I knew I had loitered in the north as long as I could.

We were both at the landing when Mark arrived. The bear was genuinely fond of the Indian, and the two romped and rolled in games I would not have undertaken. After the last dinner in the cabin that night I said, "I'm taking only the essentials, Mark. Long trip. You and Larch split what's left."

"Larch and I'll look in on the cabin once in a while. Maybe you'll send us a letter? Maybe you come back."

In the early dawn of the next day, I packed the canoe for the trip to Fort Saint James and thence to Prince George, a wild ride for more than two hundred rough miles. Mark loaded his launch and prepared for Scratch a bow seat for the long journey to Palisade Lake. When he had started his motor and seated the bear, he turned to pull away. Avoiding my eyes as he passed the canoe, he handed me a heavy willow switch. The bear looked at me as I began to paddle south. In a bound he was over the side of Mark's boat, bellowing, and swimming toward the canoe.

Tears streaming down my cheeks, I was forced to leave the thought of betrayal in the mind of the third bear. With the switch I struck him again and again across the bridge of the nose—the nose that had so often nudged me with affection and admiration. At length he turned, disbelieving, and slowly swam to Mark, who helped him aboard the launch. I heard my friend gun his engine as he turned the prow north. I paddled south with every fiber of my body. Had I ever looked back, I would never have left the northland.